"Written with the deftness, clarity, and tender grace we've come to expect from DeYoung, *What Does the Bible Really Teach about Homosexuality?* answers, point by point, the revisionist theology making inroads in even the most conservative theological circles. It is simply the very best resource any follower of Christ can have to answer the challenge of homosexuality in the church."

Gregory Koukl, President of Stand to Reason (str.org); author, *Tactics* and *Relativism*

"Solid exegesis and tight writing make this book stand out. Kevin DeYoung concisely explains the key biblical passages and clearly responds to the key objections."

Marvin Olasky, Editor in Chief, World News Group

"DeYoung takes on the most pressing issue of our day: whether we will be conformed to the spirit of the age or whether we will follow Christ. Against the sexual revolution and its high priests, DeYoung presents an alternative vision, the ancient wisdom of a Christian sexual ethic. This is the best book on this subject that I have read. Every Christian confronted with these issues, which means every Christian, should read this book. You will finish it better equipped to preach the gospel, to love the lost, to welcome the wounded, and to stand up for Jesus and his Word."

Russell D. Moore, President, The Ethics & Religious Liberty
Commission; author, *Tempted and Tried*

"Anyone looking for an accessible, reader-friendly, one-stop treatment of the biblical underpinnings of traditional Christian marriage and sexual ethics would do well to read this book. It is lucid but not simplistic, judicious but not obscure, and convicted but not shrill."

Wesley Hill, Assistant Professor of Biblical Studies, Trinity School
for Ministry; author, *Washed and Waiting: Reflections on Christian
Faithfulness and Homosexuality*

"This book provides a short, accessible, and pastoral toolbox for all Christians to navigate the shifting cultural landscape of sexuality and find confidence and hope in how the Bible directs our steps. DeYoung offers wise and readable apologetics here, providing his readers with both motive and model for how to think and talk about homosexuality and the Christian faith in a way that honors Christ and gives hope to a watching world."

Rosaria Butterfield, former tenured Professor of English at Syracuse
University; author, *The Secret Thoughts of an Unlikely Convert*;
mother, pastor's wife, and speaker

"What a gift this book is to the church! Kevin approaches the difficult question of sexuality with compassion and clarity, showing us what God's Word says about it and why it is important. Well researched, accessibly written, and gospel saturated—this, in my opinion, is now the book on this subject for our generation!"

J. D. Greear, Lead Pastor, The Summit Church, Durham,
North Carolina; author, *Jesus, Continued . . . Why the Spirit
Inside You Is Better than Jesus Beside You*

"A superb, accessible resource for lay people in every walk of life who need help making sense of one of the most critical, defining issues of our day. Kevin DeYoung approaches this highly controversial topic in a way that is biblically faithful, pastorally sensitive, historically informed, and culturally aware. The stakes are high. We cannot afford not to understand what Kevin has so helpfully laid out for us here."

Nancy Leigh DeMoss, author; radio host, *Revive Our Hearts*

"Kevin DeYoung has written a good and faithful treatment on the Bible and homosexual practice for the average churchgoer. His work addresses most of the main issues and does so in a succinct and articulate manner. I commend it."

Robert Gagnon, Associate Professor of New Testament, Pittsburgh Theological Seminary; author, *The Bible and Homosexual Practice*

"In the heated atmosphere that currently surrounds discussion of every aspect of homosexuality, the most important domain where we need careful thinking and constrained rhetoric is what the Bible does and does not say on the matter. With his customary directness and clarity, Kevin DeYoung has now met this need. For those interested in careful exegesis of the relevant passages and patient discussion of the issues that arise from it, packaged in brevity and simplicity, it would be difficult to better this book."

D. A. Carson, Research Professor of New Testament, Trinity Evangelical Divinity School

"DeYoung provides a much-needed resource that addresses the important biblical and theological issues related to homosexuality while maintaining accessibility to a broad readership. The Ten Commitments at the end of this book display DeYoung's pastoral heart and his understanding that regardless of our vices or virtues, we must preach the gospel, together strive for holiness, and exalt Christ above all things."

Christopher Yuan, Bible Teacher; speaker; author, *Out of a Far Country: A Gay Son's Journey to God*

What Does the Bible Really Teach about

Homosexuality?

Kevin DeYoung

:: **CROSSWAY**

WHEATON, ILLINOIS

What Does the Bible Really Teach about Homosexuality?

Copyright © 2015 by Kevin DeYoung

Published by Crossway
      1300 Crescent Street
      Wheaton, Illinois 60187

Cover design: Josh Dennis

Cover image: Richard Solomon Artists, Ricardo Martinez

First printing 2015

Printed in the United States of America

Trade paperback ISBN: 978-1-4335-4937-3
ePub ISBN: 978-1-4335-4940-3
PDF ISBN: 978-1-4335-4938-0
Mobipocket ISBN: 978-1-4335-4939-7

Library of Congress Cataloging-in-Publication Data
DeYoung, Kevin.
    What does the Bible really teach about homosexuality? / Kevin DeYoung.
       pages cm
    Includes bibliographical references and index.
    ISBN 978-1-4335-4937-3 (tp : alk. paper)
    1. Homosexuality—Biblical teaching. I. Title.
BS680.H67D494   2015
241'.664—dc23   2015001438

Crossway is a publishing ministry of Good News Publishers.

LB		25	24	23	22	21	20	19	18	17	16	15
13	12	11	10	9	8	7	6	5	4	3	2	

Contents

Introduction

What Does the Bible Teach about Everything?

The question "What does the Bible really teach about homo-sexuality?" is about a great many things. It's about Jesus's view of marriage, and the point of Romans 1, and the sin of Genesis 19 (whatever it was), and the abiding relevance (or not) of laws found in Leviticus. It's about the meaning of a few disputed Greek words and the significance of procreation. It's about the nature of same-sex behavior in the ancient world and whether the nature of personhood and personal fulfillment are defined by sexual expression. It's about how we change, and what can change and what cannot. It's about big themes like love and holiness and justice. It's about personal hurts and hopes and fears and longings and duties and desires. It's about faith and repentance and heaven and hell and a hundred other things.

But before we get up close to the trees, we should step back and make sure we are gazing upon the same forest. As is so often the case with controversial matters, we will never agree on the smaller subplots if it turns out we aren't even telling the same story. The Bible says *something* about homosexuality. I hope everyone can agree on at least that much. And I hope everyone can agree that the Bible is manifestly not a book *about* homosexuality. That is to say, if we think the big takeaway from this Big Book is the rightness or wrongness of homosexual activity, then we've managed to take a sublime narrative and pound it into a single talking point.

As important as the question is—"What does the Bible really teach about homosexuality?"—the first and more significant question is "What does the Bible teach about everything?" Which means we can't start this book with Leviticus 18 or Romans 1. We have to start where the Bible starts: in the beginning.

Tale as Old as Time (and Older Still)

The first person we meet in the Bible is God (Gen. 1:1). And the first thing we see about this God is that he is before all things (cf. Ps. 90:1–2). God is self-existent, independent, without beginning or end, without equal, the Creator God distinct from his creation, a holy and unrivaled God—eternal, infinite, and, in his essence, unlike anything or anyone that ever was, is, or will be. This is the God we first meet in the first verse of the first book of the Bible.

And this is the God who created all things (Neh. 9:6; Acts 14:15; 17:24). He created heaven and what is in it, the earth and what is in it, and the sea and what is in it (Rev. 10:6). What's more, he made men and women as the crown of his creation, making them in his image and after his likeness (Gen. 1:26). He created them to rule and to reproduce and to have a relationship with him (Gen. 1:26–28; cf. 3:8).

But the first man and the first woman disobeyed God's command. They listened to the Slithering One as he tempted them to doubt the clarity and goodness of God's word (Gen. 3:1–5). They took a bite from the forbidden fruit, and the fruit bit back. When sin entered the world, it was not just a fall; it was a curse. The man, the woman, the Serpent, the ground—all felt the sting of the curse so that "not the way things are supposed to be" became "the way things are." In just retribution for sin, God drove the man and the woman from the garden and placed an angel to guard the way to the tree of life (Gen. 3:24). Their heaven on earth was no more, at least not until God would bring heaven back to earth (Gen. 3:15). The central plotline of the story of Scripture was set in motion: a holy God making a way to dwell in the midst of an unholy people.

Space does not permit a full retelling of this story, but one only has to look at the Promised Land or the temple to see the same narrative carrying forward. The Promised Land was a type of Eden, and Eden was a foreshadowing of the Promised Land. God describes the creation of Israel in the same way he describes the creation of the heavens and the earth (Jer. 4:23–26; 27:5). The boundaries of Eden and the boundaries of Canaan are similar (Gen. 2:10–14; 15:18). When Jacob comes back from the east to enter Canaan, he is met by an angel (Gen. 32:22–32)—an allusion to the angel placed at the entrance to Eden. Joshua likewise encounters a heavenly guardian when approaching the Promised Land by way of Jericho (Josh. 5:13–15).

God was giving his people a new kind of paradise, a reconstituted heaven on earth, a promised land in which God would be their God and they would be his people. But once again, they proved to be covenant breakers. Generations earlier, after being expelled from the garden, God plucked Abraham out of Babylon to go to the land of Canaan (Gen. 11:31–12:7). And generations later, after being expelled from the Promised Land, God plucked his people out of Babylon and sent the exiles back to their homes (Ezra 1:1). Adam had the garden and failed to obey. Israel got the garden back, and they failed to obey. Both were expelled east of Eden. In both cases, it took the sovereign hand of God to bring his people back from Babylon to where they belonged. The Promised Land was a lens through which God's people were supposed to look back to the Eden that was and look forward to the Eden that was to come again (Heb. 11:8–10, 13–16).

In the same way, the tabernacle and the temple were meant to reflect the garden of Eden and symbolize a kind of heaven and earth. The tabernacle was a copy and shadow of what can be found in heaven (Heb. 8:5). Once inside the tent, God's people were transported into a symbolic heaven, staring at deep blue curtains with images of cherubim seeming to fly in midair (Ex. 26:1–37). The Spirit filled Bezalel and Oholiab in the fashioning of the tabernacle just as the Spirit hovered over the chaos in the formation of the heavens and the earth (Gen. 1:2; Ex. 31:2–11). The entrance to both the tabernacle and the temple was on the east, reminiscent of Eden. Angels were carved on the mercy seat on the lid of the ark of the covenant, which was placed inside the Holy of Holies—another reminder that, like Eden, angels were guarding the presence of God. Even the menorah, with its branches, buds, and blossoms, was meant to look like a tree, likely a reminder of the tree of life found in the garden (Ex. 25:31–36). The Lord God put his tabernacle in the middle of the camp (and later, his temple in the midst of the city) to visually represent his dwelling place among the people. Just as God had walked with Adam in the cool of the day, so he made a way to dwell in the midst of his chosen people.

But the temple was destroyed—divine retribution for the sins of the people. As often as God had made a way to dwell in the midst of his unholy people, just as often had they squandered their God-wrought restoration. So God sent his Son as a son of Abraham and a son of David (Matt. 1:1–17). His coming would mark a new genesis, a new beginning (Matt. 1:1). God took on flesh and tabernacled among us (John 1:14). Jesus Christ would rebuild a new temple and reform a new Israel. Jesus would be a better Moses and a second Adam (Rom. 5:12–21; 1 Cor. 15:20–28). He would die when we deserved to die (Mark 10:45). He would drink the cup of God's wrath we deserved to drink (Mark 14:36). At the same time, in death he would succeed where all others had failed, so that instead of an angel guarding the entrance to God's presence so we cannot enter in, we find an angel at the empty tomb telling us that Christ has gotten out. All the promises of God are Yes and Amen in Christ (2 Cor. 1:20). And if we repent of our sins and believe in Christ, all the promised blessings—forgiveness, cleansing, redemption, eternal life—become our promises, too (Acts 2:37–40; 16:30–31; Eph. 1:3–10; 2:1–10).

The garden, the land, and the temple did not prefigure a day when holiness no longer mattered. They pointed to the heavenly reality that has been our hope since Adam and Eve were barred from Paradise. That's why the picture of the New Jerusalem in Revelation 21 and 22 is a portrait of Eden restored. The tree of life is the long-awaited reward for those who believe and persevere. The reward is for those who know the grace of Christ (Eph. 2:1–9), are joined to Christ (Rom. 6:1–10), and have credited to their account the righteousness of Christ (2 Cor. 5:21; Phil. 3:7–11). The right to eat from the tree of life is not the right of those who profess one thing and do another (Rev. 3:1). It will not be enjoyed by those who forget their first love (2:4), those who deny the faith (2:10), or those who give themselves over to sexual immorality (2:14). Only those who overcome, only those who conquer, will be granted the right to eat of the tree of life, which is in the paradise of God (2:7). The heavenly vision of Revelation is the consummation of everything the garden, the land, and the temple pictured and predicted. No chaos, no conflict, no tears, no death, no mourning, no crying, no pain, no night, and no detestable thing. Nothing to interfere with a holy God and his holy people. The way things were—the way things should be—will finally become the way things are forever and ever.

Smaller and Bigger Than You Think

That's the story. That's what the Bible is all about. In one sense, there's not a whole lot about homosexuality. The story of the Bible is not the story of God giving a lecture on same-sex marriage or trying a case before the Supreme Court. Although homosexuality is one of the most pressing and painful controversies of our day, it's not what the church has been singing and praying and preaching about for two thousand years.

And yet, in some ways it is.

For two millennia the church has focused on worshiping a Christ who saves, a Christ who forgives, a Christ who cleanses, a Christ who challenges us and changes us, a Christ who convicts us and converts us, and a Christ who is coming again. If, as the Apostles' Creed tells us, Jesus Christ is coming again to judge the living and the dead (Acts 17:31; Rev. 19:11–21); and if those who repent of their sins and believe in Christ will live forever with God in his new creation (Mark 1:15; Acts 17:30; Rev. 21:7; 21:1–27) through the atoning work of Christ on the cross (Isa. 53:1–12; Rom. 5:1–21); and if those who are not born again (John 3:5) and do not believe in Christ (John 3:18) and do not turn from their sinful practices (1 John 3:4–10) will face eternal punishment and the just wrath of God in hell (John 3:36; 5:29); and if among those in the lake of fire excluded from the heavenly garden are the cowardly, the faithless, the detestable, murderers, the sexually immoral, sorcerers, idolaters, and all liars (Rev. 21:8, 27)—then determining what constitutes sexual immorality in God's mind has everything to do with the storyline of Scripture.

Is homosexual activity a sin that must be repented of, forsaken, and forgiven, or, given the right context and commitment, can we consider same-sex sexual intimacy a blessing worth celebrating and solemnizing?

That is the question this book seeks to answer. It's not a question that dominates the pages of the Bible. But it is a question that touches many of the important and most precious truths the Bible upholds.

What Kind of Book?

Given the highly charged nature of this topic, and considering the different sets of eyes that may be reading these words, perhaps it would be helpful to explain at the outset what kind of book this is: *this is a Christian book, with a narrow focus, defending a traditional view of marriage.* Let me develop each of those phrases.

This is a Christian book. That doesn't mean there is nothing here for non-Christians to consider. I hope that anyone interested in what the Bible says about homosexuality will be able to benefit from this book. But as a Christian writing a Christian book I am going to assume a fair amount of common ground. I'm going to treat the Bible as God's Word, as an inspired, authoritative, unbreakable, fully trustworthy account of divine revelation.[1] So whether you are a Christian leader trying to instruct others, a religious skeptic wanting to see what Scripture says, or a searching teenager trying to decide for yourself what to believe, I pray there is something in this book to help you understand the Bible a bit better.

---

[1] For more on these themes see my book *Taking God At His Word: Why the Bible Is Knowable, Necessary, and Enough* (Wheaton, IL: Crossway, 2014).

With a narrow focus. This second point follows from the first. While there is much to be gained by exploring homosexuality through the lenses of sociology, biology, history, politics, and philosophy, my aim is much simpler: to examine what the Bible teaches about same-sex behavior. Is it a sin—something always outside of God's will—when persons of the same gender experience sexual intimacy together, or can homosexual practice be holy and pleasing to God in the right circumstances?

You might have other questions you'd like this book to address: How do I tell my parents what I'm struggling with? How do I help my children with their struggles? What if I've been abused? How can I trust the church when my experience with the church has been so negative? How can I minister to my friend now that he's told me he's attracted to men? Should I attend a same-sex wedding? Should I let my lesbian daughter and her partner spend the night at my house? How can I fight against the temptation to lust? What does the Bible say about sexuality in general? How can my church minister more effectively to those with same-sex attraction? How should I speak about these issues in the public sphere? How should I handle this issue in my church and denomination? What should our policy be on hiring and ministry cooperation? How will the church help me find relational fulfillment and gospel purpose as a celibate man or woman with same-sex attraction?

These are all good questions, and there are books and blogs and new resources coming out all the time in an effort to tackle these issues. For the most part, this book is not about these questions. At least not directly. Before any of these questions can be answered, we must first figure out whether homosexual practice is a sin or a blessing or something else. Once we answer that question, we can move on to a thousand points of application and search for the most courageous and winsome ways to address the sin and suffering we all experience. Of course, at times our words will be few as we simply listen to, weep with, or put an arm around a friend. Human beings are complex creatures. There is no easy formula for shepherding a wayward soul or caring for a broken heart. But on the level of pastoral strategy and institutional discernment, our deliberations and conversations are bound to be ineffective, or even counterproductive, until we determine what the Bible teaches about the rightness or wrongness of homosexual activity. And for an increasing number of Christians, answering the question "What does the Bible really teach about homosexuality?" doesn't appear as straightforward as it once did.

Defending a traditional view of marriage. In case you didn't know already, I should make my position plain. I believe same-sex sexual intimacy is a sin. Along with most Christians around the globe and virtually every Christian in the first nineteen-and-a-half centuries of church history, I believe the Bible places homosexual behavior—no matter the level of commitment or mutual affection—in the category of sexual immorality. Why I believe this is the subject of the rest of this book.

Preaching to the Choir, but Different Choirs

At this point, candor is probably the best course of action. The elephant in the room is that there are different elephants in this room. We all come to this subject from different places with different perspectives. Let me address three types of people who may be reading this book.

First, there are the convinced. By convinced, I mean people who have opened this book certain (or at least fairly certain) that homosexual behavior is wrong. I'm going to argue for that same conclusion, but the right conclusion can be handled in the wrong way. Focusing on other people's sins, while ignoring our own, would be the wrong way. Being haughty about biblical correctness, instead of humbled by our own fallenness, would be the wrong way. Turning every conversation into a theological throwdown would be the wrong way. Treating people like projects to fix or problems to solve or points to be scored, instead of people to love, would be the wrong way. But "blessed are the pure in heart," you say. Yes, and blessed are the merciful and the mournful too. If you walk away from this book angry and arrogant, disrespectful and devoid of all empathy, someone or something has failed. I pray the failure is not mine.

Second, there are the contentious. Here I'm thinking of those whose reaction is already somewhere between simmering frustration and absolute disdain. Maybe you picked up the book wanting to get a feel for the "other" side. Maybe your friends or parents told you to read the book because they thought it might change your mind. Maybe you were hoping I'd point us in the direction of a mythical third way. I admit I may not be able to convince you to change your mind in one hundred and fifty pages. But I hope your mind will at least be open. If you are not convinced by the lexical, logical, and exegetical arguments, I only ask that you make doubly sure it is the actual arguments that are unconvincing. Our feelings matter. Our stories matter. Our friends matter. But ultimately we must search the Scriptures to see what matters most. Don't discount the messenger as a bigot if your real problem is with the Bible. I don't think I've resorted to *ad hominem* attacks, and with God as my witness, and as far as I can discern my own heart, I've not written anything in this book out of personal animus for those in the gay community. You may think I'm wrong about everything. But if affirming homosexual behavior is the more enlightened conclusion, it seems only fair that this conclusion would be reached not based on gut reactions and growing peer pressure, but by bringing the best arguments to light and weighing them out through a reasoned use of Scripture (Acts 19:9–10; 24:25).

Third, there are the confused. I will be pleased if this book can be useful for all three groups. I especially hope that something in these pages will be helpful for brothers and sisters in this last category. I'm a pastor first and foremost, and while I have tried to make an intelligent case for the historic position on marriage and sexuality, I don't pretend to have plowed new scholarly ground or overturned every stone. That's because as much as we need dense, comprehensively footnoted, five-hundred-page tomes on this subject (and we do need them), we also need resources for moms and dads and lay elders and college students and grandparents and high school administrators and small group leaders and dozens of other "ordinary" people who aren't sure how to make sense of this issue. More than anything, I want to open the Scriptures and make things a little clearer for those who may be thinking, "Something seems wrong with these new arguments, but I can't put my finger on it," or "Maybe the Bible doesn't say what I thought," or "Maybe I need to give the Bible another chance," or "All my friends are saying one thing, and I'm not sure what to believe anymore." Keep digging. Keep praying. Keep trusting that God's Word is clear, true, and good.

Odds and Ends

My outline is simple and straightforward. Part 1 consists of five chapters which examine the five most relevant and most debated biblical texts related to homosexuality. In these chapters I hope to defend biblical sexual morality, namely, that God created sex as a good gift reserved for the covenant of marriage between a man and a woman. In part 2, I focus on seven of the most common objections to this traditional view of sexual morality. These seven chapters seek to demonstrate that there are no persuasive historical, cultural, pastoral, or hermeneutical reasons for setting aside the plain meaning of the Bible as it has been understood for nearly two millennia. A concluding chapter tries to explain what is at stake in this debate.

Before we dive into the biblical texts, let me make two final preliminary comments. The first is about terms. There is no perfect way to describe the two sides in this debate, so rather than using just one set of terms I'll employ a variety of labels interchangeably. I may call the position that says homosexual behavior is sinful the *conservative* position, or the *historic* view, or the *nonaffirming* stance. Most often I'll use the term *traditional*. For the opposite view, I use words like *progressive*, *liberal*, or *affirming*. Most often I'll use the term *revisionist*. I understand these words can be misconstrued and that people on both sides won't like them for one reason or another, but I think they are all common enough to be understood.

It's also important to note that I'll be using a number of interchangeable phrases in reference to *homosexual activity*, including: *homosexual behavior*, *homosexual practice*, *same-sex sexual intimacy*, *same-sex sexual practice*, and *same-sex sexual activity*. Quite deliberately, these terms suggest a freely chosen activity or behavior. In using these terms I am not speaking in a blanket way about those who find themselves attracted to persons of the same sex, nor am I commenting on whether these desires were consciously chosen (almost certainly not) or whether and when the desires themselves are sinful. This is an important and complicated issue—exegetically, theologically, and pastorally—but it is not the focus of this book (for a brief discussion see "Appendix 2: Same-Sex Attraction: Three Building Blocks"). Unless specifically stated otherwise, it should be assumed that in speaking of homosexuality I am talking about the self-determined activity of those who are engaged in sexual behavior with persons of the same sex. If my writing sounds more attuned to men who practice homosexuality, that's because the Bible is calibrated in the same way. The experience of women who practice homosexuality can be quite different from that of men, but the same determination about the activity itself applies equally to both sexes, even if the Bible leans more heavily in helping us understand men-with-men sexual behavior.

Along those lines, I've tried to avoid the labels *gay* and *lesbian* because I think they add confusion rather than clarity to the question at hand. In a few instances where the terms are employed, I've added a description like "those who self-identify as gay or lesbian." Similarly, although I do not believe two persons of the same sex actually can be married (according to the biblical and traditional understanding of the word *marriage*), I do refer to *same-sex marriage*. I chose to clearly state my objection up front rather than put "same-sex marriage" in quotations marks throughout the book or refer to it as *so-called* same-sex marriage.

My final introductory comment concerns the authority of Scripture. It's become cliché to hold up the Bereans as an example of biblical studiousness, but in this case it's a cliché worth perpetuating. When Paul preached the Word in Thessalonica, people were so angry they formed a mob, beat up his friends, and drove Paul and his companions out of the city (Acts 17:5–9). Paul's experience in Berea, however, was much different: "Now these Jews were more noble than those in Thessalonica; they received the word with all eagerness, examining the Scriptures daily to see if these things were so" (Acts 17:11). I want to be like the Bereans, and I hope you do, too. Let's be eager and careful and persistent in studying the Word. On any subject, in any direction, we must be careful not to twist the Word to suit our own whims and wishes. As painful as it can be, we must reinterpret our experiences through the Word of

God, rather than let our experiences dictate what the Bible can and cannot mean.

If Jesus thought the Scriptures were spoken by God himself (Matt. 19:4–5) and utterly unbreakable (John 10:35), it's certainly appropriate in any confusing, complicated, or controversial matter to ask at the very outset, "What does the Bible really teach?" Whether you are prepared to agree or disagree with this book, I encourage you to keep three things open: your head, your heart, and your Bible. Don't settle for slogans and put-downs. Don't assume the worst about those who disagree with you. And don't think that God won't speak to you through the Scriptures if you stay humble, honest, and hungry for the truth. After all, man does not live by bread alone (or sex alone), but by every word that comes from the mouth of God (Deut. 8:3; Matt. 4:4).

Part 1

UNDERSTANDING GOD'S WORD

1

One Man, One Woman, One Flesh

GENESIS 1–2

Suppose God wanted to create a world in which marriage required a man and a woman. How would he arrange this world? What sort of story would be told?

Perhaps he would first make the man, and then—seeing the man was all alone—make a suitable partner for him. Maybe, in an expression of their equality and complementarity, God would fashion the second human being out of the first. Maybe the name of the one (*woman, ishah* in Hebrew) would be derived from her natural complement (*man, ish* in Hebrew). And in order to show the unique fittedness of the man for the woman, perhaps God would give them a command (to be fruitful and multiply) that could only be fulfilled by the coming together of the two sexes. Maybe the story would end with the two—one man and one woman—starting a new family together and entering into a new covenant relationship, solemnized by an oath and sealed by the sort of physical union capable of perpetuating this family and reflecting their status as image bearers of a divine Creator.

If God wanted to establish a world in which the normative marital and sexual relationship is that between persons of the opposite sex, Genesis 1–2 fits perfectly. The narrative strongly suggests what the church has almost uniformly taught: "Marriage is to be between one man and one woman."[1] A different marital arrangement requires an entirely different creation account, one with two men or two women, or at least the absence of any hints of gender complementarity and procreation. It's hard not to conclude from a straightforward reading of Genesis 1–2 that the divine design for sexual intimacy is not any combination of persons, or even any type of two persons coming together, but one man becoming one flesh with one woman.

In recent years, however, some have questioned whether this straightforward reading of the text is really all that straightforward. Eve, some argue, was not a complement to Adam as much as a basic companion. The problem she remedied was aloneness, not incompleteness. And doesn't the text indicate that the woman, as opposed to the animals, was suitable for the man because she was *like* the man, not because she was different? Perhaps the language of "one flesh" does not depend on any particular sex act (or any sex act at all). After all, Laban told Jacob "you are my bone and my flesh!" (Gen. 29:14), and the tribes of Israel told David "we are your bone and flesh" (2 Sam. 5:1; cf. Judg. 9:2; 2 Sam. 19:12–13; 1 Chron. 11:1). Why make so much of some supposed sexual "fittedness" when Genesis 2 nowhere mentions procreation? To be sure, the argument goes,

---

[1] *Westminster Confession of Faith* (WCF) 24.1. This confession (1646) has been used by Reformed and Presbyterian churches for centuries and serves as a doctrinal standard for millions of Christians around the world.

Genesis uses the example of a man and a woman forming the covenant bond of marriage, but why can't this illustrate what is normal rather than prescribe what is normative? The union of two men or two women can demonstrate the same leaving and cleaving and the same intimate sharing of all things that we see from Adam and Eve in Genesis 2.

As plausible as this revisionist reading might look at first glance, it does not do justice to the specific contours of the creation account. There are at least five reasons we are right to think that Genesis 1–2 establishes God's design for marriage and that this design requires one man and one woman.

First, the way in which the woman was created indicates that she is the man's divinely designed complement. In Genesis 2:21, we see the Lord God taking something from the man (one of his ribs) in order to make a helper suitable for him (v. 18). Then verse 22 emphasizes that the woman was not fashioned out of thin air or out of the dust of the ground, but from "the rib that the Lord God had taken from the man." What makes the woman unique is both that she is like the man (expressed in the covenantal commitment statement "bone of my bones and flesh of my flesh") *and* that she is differentiated from the man. The text has sameness and difference in view. Adam delights that the woman is not another animal *and* not another man. She is exactly what the man needs: a suitable helper, equal to the man but also his opposite. She is an *ishah* taken out of *ish,* a new creation fashioned from the side of man to be something other than a man (2:23).

Second, the nature of the one-flesh union presupposes two persons of the opposite sex. The phrase "one flesh" points to sexual intimacy, as suggested by the reference to nakedness in verse 25. That's why Paul uses the language of "one flesh" when warning the Corinthians against being "joined" to a prostitute (1 Cor. 6:15–16). The act of sexual intercourse brings a man and a woman together as one relationally *and* organically. The sameness of the parts in same-sex activity does not allow for the two to become one in the same way. Mere physical contact—like holding hands or sticking your finger in someone's ear—does not unite two people in an organic union, nor does it bring them together as a single subject to fulfill a biological function.[2] When Genesis 2:24 begins with "Therefore" (or, "For this reason"), it connects the intimacy of becoming one flesh (v. 24) with the complementarity of Woman being taken out of Man (v. 23). The *ish* and the *ishah* can become one flesh because theirs is not just a sexual union but a *re*union, the bringing together of two differentiated beings, with one made *from* and both made *for* the other.[3]

Third, only two persons of the opposite sex can fulfill the procreative purposes of marriage. One of the reasons it was not good for the man to be alone is because by himself he could not reflect the Creator's creative designs for the world. God created vegetation, trees, fish, birds, and every living creature "according to their kind" (Gen. 1:11, 12, 21, 24, 25). The multiplication of the plant and animal world was to take place each according to its own type. Likewise, God created the man and the woman deliberately so that they could be fruitful and multiply (1:28). If the man was to fulfill this command, God would have to make "a helper fit for him" (2:18). While it's true that procreation is not explicitly mentioned in Genesis 2, it is directly commanded in Genesis 1 and specifically mentioned as affected by the fall in Genesis 3. Clearly, we are meant to

---

[2] Patrick Lee and Robert P. George, *Conjugal Union: What Marriage Is and Why It Matters* (New York: Cambridge University Press, 2014), 50.

[3] See Robert A. J. Gagnon, *The Bible and Homosexual Practice: Texts and Hermeneutics* (Nashville, TN: Abingdon, 2001), 60–63. Along the same lines, John Calvin observes, "Something was taken from Adam, in order that he might embrace, with greater benevolence, a part of himself. He lost, therefore, one of his ribs; but, instead of it, a far richer reward was granted him, since he obtained a faithful associate of life; for he now saw himself, who had before been imperfect, rendered complete in his wife" (*Commentaries on the First Book of Moses Called Genesis,* vol. 1, trans. John King [Grand Rapids, MI: Baker, 1989], 133).

see offspring issuing from the union of the uniquely fitted *ish* and *ishah*. That sometimes married men and women are unable to have children by reason of biological infirmity or old age does not change the procreative purpose of marriage found in Genesis. Marriage is, by definition, that sort of union from which—if all the plumbing is working properly—children can be conceived. Homosexual unions by their very nature do not meet this definition, nor can they fulfill this procreative purpose. The issue is not, as one revisionist author argues, whether procreation is required for a marriage to be valid.[4] The issue is whether marriage—by nature, by design, and by aim—is a covenant between two persons whose one-flesh commitment is the sort of union which produces offspring.

The importance of procreation as the natural outworking of the marriage covenant is also seen in the Old Testament levirate laws. These laws, like the one in Deuteronomy 25:5–6 (cf. Mark 12:19), are so named because they obligate a deceased's man's brother to marry his widowed sister-in-law (if she is childless) and produce offspring for his brother. Reproduction was so plainly the normal expectation (and blessing) of marriage that even death could not be allowed to thwart marriage's procreative purposes under the Mosaic law-covenant.

We see this principle even more clearly in Malachi 2:15:

> Did he not make them one, with a portion of the Spirit in their union? And what was the one God seeking? Godly offspring. So guard yourselves in your spirit, and let none of you be faithless to the wife of your youth.

The Hebrew in this verse is among the most difficult in the entire Old Testament, so we cannot be overly dogmatic about any interpretation, but the English Standard Version reflects the consensus

---

[4] James V. Brownson, *Bible, Gender, Sexuality: Reframing the Church's Debate on Same-Sex Relationships* (Grand Rapids, MI: Eerdmans, 2013), 115.

of most translations (including the Holman Christian Standard Bible, King James Version, New International Version, New Living Translation, and New Revised Standard Version). Malachi, in rebuking the men of Judah for treating their wives faithlessly, deliberately harkens back to the creation account. He says in effect, "God made the man and the woman to become one flesh so they might produce godly offspring. Be on guard, therefore, that you not profane such a holy union by divorcing your wives." Not only does Malachi recognize the procreative purpose in marriage; he finds this principle in the Genesis creation account. This is why the *Westminster Confession* (Presbyterian/Reformed) says marriage was given, in part, for the "increase" of "holy seed," and the *Book of Common Prayer* (Anglican) says holy matrimony was "ordained for the procreation of children," and *Humanae Vitae* (Catholic) says "the unitive significance and the procreative significance" are "both inherent to the marriage act."[5] While it would be wrong to say procreation is the *sole* purpose in marriage or that sexual intimacy is given *only* as a means to some reproductive end, it would also be wrong to think marriage can be properly defined without any reference to the offspring that should (and normally does) result from the one-flesh union of a husband and wife.

Fourth, Jesus himself reinforces the normativity of the Genesis account. When asked to weigh in on the Jewish divorce debate—whether divorce was permissible for any cause or whether only sexual sin could tear asunder the marriage covenant—Jesus sides with the more conservative Shammai school and disallows divorce for any cause except sexual immorality. To make his point, Jesus first reminds his audience that God "from the beginning made them male and female" and then quotes directly from Genesis 2:24 (Matt. 19:4–6; Mark 10:6–9). There is no

---

[5] WCF 24.2; *Book of Common Prayer*, "The Form of Solemnization of Matrimony"; *Humanae Vitae* 2.12.

indication that Jesus references Genesis for mere illustrative purposes. In Jesus's mind, to answer the divorce question necessitates a right understanding of marriage, and to get at the nature of marriage one must go back to the beginning, where we see God instituting marriage as the lifelong union of a man and a woman. Moreover, monogamy makes sense only within this Genesis understanding of marriage. Apart from the complementarity of the two sexes there is no moral logic which demands that marriage should be restricted to a twosome.[6] I'm not arguing that the acceptance of same-sex marriage will lead inexorably to the acceptance of polygamy. But once you've accepted the former, you no longer have a consistent intellectual case to reject the latter. It is mere sentiment and lingering tradition which leads many progressives to insist that same-sex unions ought to involve the commitment of two persons and only two persons. If marriage is simply the formation of a kinship bond between those who are committed wholly to one another, there is no reason why multiple persons or groups of people cannot commit themselves wholly to one another. There is no internal coherence to the notions of monogamy and exclusivity if marriage is something other than the reunion of two complementary and differentiated sexes. It's because God made the woman *from* the man that she is also *for* the man (1 Cor. 11:8–9, 11–12). And it's because the two—male and female—are divinely designed complements each for the other that monogamy makes sense and same-sex marriage does not.

---

[6] True, polygamy existed in the Old Testament, but it does not enter the picture as a divine blessing (Gen. 4:23–24) and never receives divine approval (see Denny Burk, *What Is the Meaning of Sex?* [Wheaton, IL: Crossway, 2013], 98–100). Polygamy is often the source of pain and heartache in the Old Testament and in the New Testament is ruled out by both Jesus (Matt. 19:3–9; Mark 10:1–12; cf. Matt. 5:31–32) and Paul (1 Cor. 7:2; 1 Tim. 3:2; Titus 1:6). But even where polygamy was practiced, the two-ness of the marital bond still found expression. Solomon's wives were not married to each other. The nature of marriage was still a man and a woman in one-flesh union, even if the man joined with many women separately in multiple marriages. It is important to emphasize Jesus's assumption and methodology, to the effect that polygamy should be prohibited precisely because it fails to line up with God's design in the garden.

Fifth, the redemptive-historical significance of marriage as a divine symbol in the Bible only works if the marital couple is a complementary pair. Think about the complementary nature of creation itself. In the beginning, God created the heavens and the earth (Gen. 1:1). And not only that, but within this cosmic pairing, we find other "couples": the sun and the moon, morning and evening, day and night, the sea and the dry land, plants and animals, and finally, at the apex of the creation, the man and his wife. In every pairing, each part belongs with the other but neither is interchangeable. Just as heaven and earth were created to be together—and, indeed, that's how the whole story of the Bible ends—so marriage is to be a symbol of this divine design: two differentiated entities uniquely fitted for one another.[7]

It makes perfect sense, then, that the coming together of heaven and earth in Revelation 21–22 is preceded by the marriage supper of the Lamb in Revelation 19. Marriage was created as a picture of the fittedness of heaven and earth, or as Ephesians 5 puts it, of Christ and the church (vv. 31–32). The meaning of marriage is more than mutual sacrifice and covenantal commitment. Marriage, by its very nature, requires complementarity. The mystical union of Christ and the church—each "part" belonging to the other but neither interchangeable—cannot be pictured in marital union without the differentiation of male and female. If God wanted us to conclude that men and woman were interchangeable in the marriage relationship, he not only gave us the wrong creation narrative; he gave us the wrong *meta*narrative. Homosexuality simply does not fit with the created order in Genesis 1 and 2. And with these two chapters as the foundation upon which the rest of the redemptive-historical story is built, we'll see that homosexual behavior does not fit in with the rest of the Bible either.

---

[7] See N. T. Wright's Humanum 2014 lecture for more on this theme (available on YouTube, accessed December 4, 2014, http://www.youtube.com/watch?v=AsB-JDsOTwE).

2

Those Infamous Cities

GENESIS 19

You will not find two more infamous cities in all the Bible than Sodom and Gomorrah. In Genesis 19 the Lord rained on them sulfur and fire, a devastating punishment for their brazen wickedness. Throughout the rest of the Old Testament, Sodom and Gomorrah are synonymous with extreme sinfulness (Isa. 1:9–10; 3:9; Jer. 23:14; Ezek. 16:44–58) and divine judgment (Deut. 29:23; Isa. 13:19; Jer. 49:18; 50:40; Lam. 4:6; Amos 4:11; Zeph. 2:9). In the New Testament, Jesus often references Sodom and (less frequently) Gomorrah in an effort to warn the people of impending wrath and expose their hardness of heart (Matt. 10:14–15; 11:23–24; Luke 10:10–12; 17:26–30). Even in our day, the two cities are a byword for sin and judgment. Several years ago one cultural critic suggested that as a country we were slouching toward Gomorrah.[1] Our word *sodomy* comes from the type of sin attempted at Sodom.

---

[1] Robert H. Bork, *Slouching Towards Gomorrah: Modern Liberalism and American Decline*, (New York: Regan Books, 1996).

Everyone agrees that the story in Genesis 19 is horrifying. Two strangers meet Lot (Abraham's nephew) at the gate of Sodom. Lot convinces the men, who are actually angels, to stay with him at his house. After a meal and before they could retire for the night, the men of Sodom, both young and old, surround Lot's house and demand to have sex with the two travelers.[2] After Lot refuses to bring out his guests (and tragically, offers his virgin daughters instead), the mob grows even more unruly. But just as they press against Lot to break the door down, the two guests bring Lot into the house and strike the men of Sodom with blindness (vv. 1–11). Although they didn't get to follow through with their crime, the men of Sodom did more than enough to earn their infamous reputation.

But what exactly was the sin committed (or attempted) by the men of Sodom? Genesis 19 is about violent gang rape, hardly a picture of two men entering into a consensual and covenantal sexual relationship. Are we sure the punishment of Sodom and Gomorrah had anything to do with homosexuality? In the longest post-Genesis passage related to Sodom, social justice seems to be the concern. "Behold," Ezekiel writes, "this was the guilt of your sister Sodom: she and her daughters had pride, excess of food, and prosperous ease, but did not aid the poor and needy" (Ezek. 16:49). It's no wonder revisionist authors argue that the sin of Sodom was chiefly (solely?) a lack of hospitality. Even one well-respected scholar in the nonaffirming camp has dismissed the whole story of Sodom and Gomorrah as "irrelevant to the topic" of homosexuality.[3] Maybe the traditional understanding of these infamous cities has been

---

[2] The text says the men of Sodom demanded to "know" the men staying with Lot (Gen. 19:5). In Genesis, the Hebrew verb "to know" (*yada*) is often used as a euphemism for sexual intercourse (4:1, 17, 25; 24:16). Clearly, this is how the word is used a few verses later when Lot says that his daughters "have not known any man" (19:8).

[3] Richard B. Hays, *The Moral Vision of the New Testament: A Contemporary Introduction to New Testament Ethics* (New York: HarperOne, 1996), 381.

mistaken. Maybe the same-sex reading was manufactured by Philo and Josephus in the first century. Maybe the sin of Sodom should have no bearing on what we think about committed homosexual relationships today.

Upon Further Review

Despite the initial plausibility of rereading Genesis 19 in this revisionist way, there are several reasons why we are right to see homosexual practice as one aspect of Sodom's sin and as a reason Sodom and Gomorrah were destroyed.

(1) The reference to Sodom in Ezekiel 16 supports the traditional notion that Sodom's sin—at least one aspect of it—was sexual in nature. Look again at Ezekiel 16:49, this time with a little more of the context.

> Not only did you walk in their ways and do according to their abominations; within a very little time you were more corrupt than they in all your ways. As I live, declares the Lord God, your sister Sodom and her daughters have not done as you and your daughters have done. Behold, this was the guilt of your sister Sodom: she and her daughters had pride, excess of food, and prosperous ease, but did not aid the poor and needy. They were haughty and did an abomination before me. So I removed them, when I saw it. (16:47–50)

The word *abomination* translates the Hebrew word *to'ebah*. The "abomination" in verse 50 is a separate, specific sin that the Lord has in mind, but it is also one of the several "abominations" referenced in verse 47. The same word is used in Leviticus 18:22 and 20:13, where a man lying with a male as with a woman is called an abomination (*to'ebah*). Several sins in the Holiness Code of Leviticus are described as abominations, but only this one is singled out by itself as an abomination. The use of *to'ebah* in Ezekiel, with reference to Sodom's sin, is an echo of Leviticus 18 and 20. Sodom's sins were many: pride, social injustice, *and* pursuing homosexual behavior.

(2) Literature from Second Temple Judaism (the time between the reconstruction of the temple in 516 BC and the final destruction of the temple in AD 70) shows that Sodom's reputation for same-sex behavior cannot be explained as a first-century invention by Philo or Josephus. Consider, for example, the following passages, all from the second century BC:

> But you, my children, shall not be like that: In the firmament, in the earth, in the sea, in all the products of his workmanship discern the Lord who made all things, so that you do not become like Sodom, which departed from the order of nature. Likewise the Watchers departed from nature's order; the Lord pronounced a curse on them at the Flood. (*T. Naph.* 3:4–5)

> From the words of Enoch the Righteous I tell you that you will be sexually promiscuous like the promiscuity of the Sodomites and will perish, with few exceptions. (*T. Benj.* 9:1)

> And in that month the Lord executed the judgment of Sodom and Gomorrah and Zeboim and all of the district of the Jordan. And he burned them with fire and sulphur and he annihilated them till this day just (as he said), "Behold, I have made known to you all of their deeds that (they were) cruel and great sinners and they were polluting themselves and they were fornicating in their flesh and they were causing pollution upon the earth." And thus the Lord will execute judgment like the judgment of Sodom on places where they act according to the pollution of Sodom. (*Jub.* 16:5)[4]

---

[4] James H. Charlesworth, ed., *The Old Testament Pseudepigrapha*, 2 vols. (Peabody, MA: Hendrickson, 2009 [1983], 1.812; 1.827; 2.35, respectively). See also Thomas E. Schmidt, *Straight*

In all three examples Sodom is an example of egregious sexual sin. The language of fornicating *and* of "polluting themselves" in *Jubilees* suggests that Sodom's sexual transgression was of a unique kind—not merely fornication, but also something more polluting. Likewise, the *Testament of Naphtali* speaks of Sodom's departure from "the order of nature." True, the text also speaks of the angelic "Watchers" (i.e., the Nephilim in Genesis 6) departing from nature's order in having sex with the daughters of men, but this is by way of comparison (not necessarily identification) with Sodom's sin. The *Testament of Naphtali* admonishes that "you do not become like Sodom." It makes more sense, therefore, for the sin in question to be homosexual activity rather than sex with angels. Surely, the former was more of a real possibility in the surrounding culture than the latter.

The bottom line: Sodom had a reputation for more than social injustice. The city was a byword for sexual sin, and likely for homosexual sin. Graffiti in Pompeii, which was destroyed by volcanic eruption in 79 AD, indicates a thriving homosexual subculture in that small city. Amidst the graffiti—which, on the level of sophomoric crudeness, is akin to what you might expect to read in a dirty gas station bathroom—is a reference to "Sodom and Gomorrah," apparently written by a Jew or an early Christian who equated the practice of homosexuality with the sins of those biblical cities.[5]

(3) Most importantly, Sodom and Gomorrah are associated with homosexual practice in the New Testament. Jude 7 says, "Sodom and Gomorrah and the surrounding cities, which likewise indulged in sexual immorality and pursued unnatural desire, serve as an example by undergoing a punishment of eter-

---

and Narrow? Compassion and Clarity in the Homosexuality Debate (Downers Grove, IL: InterVarsity Press, 1995), 88–89.
[5] Found in Thomas K. Hubbard, ed., *Homosexuality in Greece and Rome: A Sourcebook of Basic Documents* (Berkeley, CA: University of California Press, 2003), 384, 422–23.

nal fire." The phrase "unnatural desire" (*sarkos heteras*) could be translated literally as "other flesh," leading some scholars to argue that the sin in view is having sex with angels. This interpretation is possible, but it's better to take "other flesh" as a reference to men lying with a male instead of a female (as per the Mosaic law in Lev. 18:22 and 20:13). It would be hard to hold the men of Sodom accountable for pursuing sex with angels when they had no idea the guests with Lot were angelic beings. Moreover, according to Jude, "the surrounding cities . . . likewise indulged" in the sin of pursuing *sarkos heteras*. Are we to think the other towns in the area also pursued sex with angels? It's more plausible to conclude that the sin designated by "other flesh" is the sin of homosexual activity.

To be sure, the scene in Genesis 19 looks very different from two men or two women entering into a consensual and committed sexual relationship. The case against same-sex sexual intimacy is less obvious from the Sodom and Gomorrah account than from the other passages we will consider. And yet, the destruction of these infamous cities is not irrelevant to the matter at hand. From the allusion in Ezekiel, to the perception of Sodom in other Jewish literature, to the mention of unnatural desire in Jude, we see that Sodom had a reputation for sexual sin in general and homosexual sin in particular. While the violence associated with homosexual behavior in Sodom certainly made the offense worse, the nature of the act itself contributed to the overwhelmingly negative assessment of the city. Sodom and Gomorrah were guilty of a great many sins; we don't have to prove that homosexual practice was the only sin to show that it was one of them.

3

Taking a Strange Book Seriously

LEVITICUS 18, 20

Two verses in Leviticus speak directly to the issue of homosexuality:

> You shall not lie with a male as with a woman; it is an abomination. (18:22)

> If a man lies with a male as with a woman, both of them have committed an abomination; they shall surely be put to death; their blood is upon them. (20:13)

Not surprisingly, these two verses have generated a lot of controversy in recent years. In particular, two broad questions must be answered about these prohibitions: First, what sin is forbidden by Leviticus 18:22 and 20:13? And second, do these commands have any abiding significance for Christians no longer bound by the Mosaic law-covenant?

What Sin?

In order to answer the first question, let's back up a bit and understand the big idea in Leviticus. The word *holy* or *holiness* occurs eighty-seven times in Leviticus. Holiness is the book's overarching theme. The whole system of Israel's worship assumed the holiness of God as its starting place. You have holy people (the priests), with holy clothes, in a holy land (Canaan), at a holy place (tabernacle), using holy utensils and holy objects, celebrating holy days, living by a holy law, that they might be a kingdom of priests and a holy nation.

The second half of Leviticus, from chapter 17 onward, is sometimes called the Holiness Code because it details how the Israelites were to live as God's holy people. Leviticus 19:2 gives the underlying command and motivation: "You shall be holy, for I the LORD your God am holy." Chapter 18 is about holiness as it relates to the family and sexual activity. Leviticus 18 doesn't tell us everything we need to know about sex, but it gives us the basic rules: incest is bad (vv. 6–27); taking a rival wife is bad (v. 18); coming in contact with menstrual uncleanness is bad (v. 19); adultery is bad (v. 20); killing our children is bad (v. 21); homosexual activity is bad (v. 22); and bestiality is bad (v. 23). If God's people became unclean by these things, they would be driven from the land just like the nations before them had been vomited out (vv. 24–30).

The question about the kind of homosexuality prohibited by the Holiness Code is relatively straightforward. The other laws against sexual sin in Leviticus 18 are not qualified in any way. We find no hints that incest could be acceptable if it took place between consenting adults or that bestiality could be appropriate so long as the men and women did not throw off their gendered identity. There is no more reason in the text to qualify the prohibition against homosexuality than to qualify any of the other sexual sins. In fact, that Leviticus 18 spends so much time carefully delineating which sexual relationships are sinfully too "close" and therefore incestuous (vv. 6–17) suggests that no such parsing is necessary with respect to homosexuality because the condemnation is absolute. Where homosexuality is condemned among the Assyrians or the Hittites, it is often condemned in specific terms for a specific act (e.g., a man violating his son).[1] And yet, there is no suggestion in Leviticus that we are talking about only a narrow type of homosexual behavior.

Just as crucially, the sin in Leviticus 18:22 and 20:13 is described in a way that harkens back to the created order. The text says nothing about an older man and a youth. It uses the generic language of "male," stipulating that a man shall not lie with a male as with a woman. The phrase "as with a woman" is significant. It calls to mind Genesis 2, where God made the first woman from the side of the man that she might be his helper and his unique complement. The reason for the prohibitions against homosexual behavior in the Mosaic law, and the reason the prohibitions are stated so absolutely, is because men were designed to have sex with women, not a man with another male. The key consideration (really the only one mentioned in the text) is the gender of those engaged in sexual activity. Whether the participants were willing or of age does not come into play. It's likely that Leviticus 20:13—with the language "both of them have committed an abomination"—is a euphemistic way of condemning both the active and passive roles in homosexual behavior.

Likewise, the prohibitions against homosexual behavior

---

[1] Gordon J. Wenham, "The Old Testament Attitude to Homosexuality," *Expository Times* 102, no. 9 (1991): 360–61.

cannot be reduced to victimization categories. After all, *both* parties were to receive the death penalty. The Mosaic law prescribed no punishment for a woman forcibly seized by a man (Deut. 22:25–26). If this were a question of homosexual rape (at the hands of a master, or a conquering army, or a violent mob), only the aggressor would be put to death. Leviticus is doing more than outlaw unwanted same-sex sexual behavior.

Israel was to be holy because Yahweh was holy. As a holy nation, God's people were to be different from the surrounding peoples and cultures—which entailed a radically different sexual ethic. And that meant an absolute prohibition against homosexual behavior of every kind.[2] God's plan for sexual intimacy in the garden was one man with one woman—not close relatives, not the wife of another man, not a man and an animal, and not two men or two women. The pattern we saw in Genesis is the pattern we see reflected in the Holiness Code in Leviticus.

Still Relevant?

If the first question had to do with the sin prohibited in Leviticus 18:22 and 20:13, the second question has to do with the significance of these prohibitions. So what if Leviticus says homosexual practice is wrong? Leviticus says a lot of goofy things. What about charging interest on a loan? What about wearing clothes with two kinds of fabric? What about eating bacon? What about having sex with your wife during her monthly period? Aren't we guilty of picking and choosing which commands still matter? How can two little verses, in a book full of commands we constantly ignore, have any abiding relevance for the church today?

Let me suggest six reasons why we cannot set aside Leviti-

---

[2] Although Leviticus mentions only male homosexuality, lesbianism (if known at the time) certainly would have been forbidden by necessary implication.

cus 18:22 and 20:13 but should view these prohibitions as an expression of God's unchanging moral will.

(1) No disciple of Jesus should start with the presumption that the Mosaic commands are largely irrelevant. Jesus himself insisted that he did not come to abolish the tiniest speck from the Law (Matt. 5:17–18). Jesus spoke of fulfilling the Old Testament Scripture but never of casually dispensing with it. To be sure, discipleship under the new covenant is different from life under the old. All foods have been declared clean (Mark 7:19; Acts 10:8–11:18); holy days have been rendered optional (Rom. 14:5–6); the entire sacrificial system of temple, priest, and sacrifice has been superseded (Heb. 7:1–10:18). Jesus brings the Scripture to completion, to its climax, to its intended goal. This is far different, however, from assuming that unfamiliar sections in Leviticus should be automatically set aside. In the truest sense, *nothing* in the Old Testament should be set aside. All Scripture has been breathed out by God and is profitable for the Christian (2 Tim. 3:16–17). Even the obsolete sacrificial system still teaches us about the nature of spiritual worship and true discipleship (Rom. 12:1–2). Every law in the Old Testament reveals something about God's character and the nature of our obedience. If the underlying principle from Leviticus 18:22 and 20:13 is something other than "God does not approve of homosexual behavior," then that needs to be proven from Scripture, not simply asserted based on a casual dismissal of Old Testament instruction.

(2) There is no indication in the New Testament that Leviticus should be treated as particularly obscure or peripheral. Quite the contrary. Jesus referred to Leviticus 19:18 ("Love your neighbor as yourself") more than any other verse in the Old Testament, and the New Testament refers to it ten times. Likewise, both Peter and Paul quoted Leviticus as part of their summons to holiness (2 Cor. 6:16, quoting Lev. 26:12;

1 Pet. 1:16, quoting Lev. 11:44). The authors of the New Testament did not hesitate to turn to Leviticus, the preeminent book on holiness in their Bibles, to find instruction and exhortation for godly living. In 1 Corinthians 5, Paul appeals directly to the law of Moses—Leviticus 18:8; Deuteronomy 22:30; 27:20—to establish the sinfulness of incest (a move he makes again in 1 Corinthians 6 with respect to homosexuality). Paul found in Leviticus moral obligations still binding on the Christian. The sexual ethic of the Old Testament was not abrogated like the sacrificial system, but carried forward into the early church. The law is good if one uses it lawfully (1 Tim. 1:8).

(3) Paul's term for "men who practice homosexuality" (1 Cor. 6:9; 1 Tim. 1:10) was derived from two words—*arsēn* (man) and *koitē* (bed)—found in Leviticus 18:22 and 20:13 (Septuagint). There are no instances of the word (*arsenokoitai*) prior to Paul. Even many revisionist scholars agree that Paul coined the term from Leviticus (see chap. 5 for the full discussion). There may also be an allusion to the verdict of Leviticus 20:13 ("both of them have committed an abomination") in Romans 1:24 ("God gave them up . . . to the dishonoring of their bodies among themselves").

(4) Leviticus uses strong language in denouncing homosexual behavior, calling it "an abomination." Outside of Leviticus, the Hebrew word *to'ebah* appears forty-three times in Ezekiel and sixty-eight times in the rest of the Old Testament, usually with respect to especially grievous sins.[3] We cannot reduce *to'ebah* to a mere social taboo or ritual uncleanness. The word generally signifies something the Lord despises. "There are six things the LORD hates," Proverbs declares, "seven that are an abomination to him" (6:16; cf. Deut. 12:31). As revisionist authors are quick to point out, all the sexual sins in Le-

---

[3] See Robert A. J. Gagnon, *The Bible and Homosexual Practice: Texts and Hermeneutics* (Nashville, TN: Abingdon, 2001), 117–20.

viticus 18 are lumped together under the term "abominations" (vv. 26–27, 29–30), but only male-with-male sex is singled out by itself as an abomination. In fact, it is the only forbidden act given this label in the entire Holiness Code. The death penalty, for both parties, also speaks to the seriousness of the offense in God's eyes.

(5) The reference to a woman's menstrual period (18:19; 20:18) should not call into question the rest of the sexual ethic described in Leviticus 18 and 20. For starters, there is a clear progression in both chapters of sexual sin deviating in increasing measure from the design of male-female monogamy. In Leviticus 18:19–23, the offenses move from sex with a menstruating woman, to sex with your neighbor's wife, to sex with another male, to sex with an animal. Each new offense moves another step away from God's design. Likewise, in Leviticus 20:10–16, the offenses move from sex with your neighbor's wife, to sex with a family member, to sex with a family member of a younger generation, to sex with another man, to sex with more than one partner, to sex with an animal, to a woman taking the role of a man in approaching an animal to have sex with it. Having sex during a woman's menstrual uncleanness is the lowest rung of the ladder in chapter 18 and not part of the progression at all in chapter 20.

Moreover, we have to understand what the Old Testament means by "uncleanness." Leviticus 18:19 forbids a husband from having sex with his wife during the time where blood is being discharged, for this would render him unclean from her uncleanness. The question, then, is whether menstruation still makes a woman unclean. Menstruation was not a sin (no sacrifice was required to atone for it). It was a matter of ritual uncleanness. But with the coming of Christ—and the elimination of the sacrificial system, the temple, and the Levitical priesthood—the whole system which required ritual cleanness has been removed. In the Old Testament, not all uncleanness was sin, but all sin made you unclean. As Jonathan Klawans notes in *The Jewish Study Bible*, ritual impurity and moral impurity are two analogous yet distinct categories.[4] Cleanness still matters in the New Testament, but it becomes an exclusively moral category instead of a ritual one. Cleanness refers to those acts that are morally pure in God's eyes, which is why the faith of the menstruating women in Luke 8 is more important than her twelve years of bleeding (vv. 43–48). The lesson from Leviticus 18:19 is not "throw out the whole chapter," but "refrain from whatever sexual activity makes you unclean."

(6) Apart from the question of sex during menstruation, the sexual ethic in Leviticus 18 and 20 is squarely reaffirmed in the New Testament. Adultery is still a sin (Matt. 5:27–30). Incest is still a sin (1 Cor. 5:1–13).[5] Even polygamy is more clearly rejected (1 Cor. 7:2; 1 Tim. 3:2). It would be strange for the prohibition against homosexual practice to be set aside when the rest of the sexual ethic is not, especially considering how the rejection of same-sex behavior is rooted in the created order.

The case against the abiding significance of Leviticus sounds compelling at first, but the arguments often amount to little more than sloganeering. Anyone who has studied the Bible as a serious discipline understands that navigating the relationship between the Old and the New Testament can be tricky business. We don't simply adopt the Mosaic covenant as our church membership covenant. Nor do we simply dismiss God's gracious self-disclosure in the Torah because of a gag line about

---

[4] Jonathan Klawans, "Concepts of Purity in the Bible," in *The Jewish Study Bible*, ed. Adele Berlin and Marc Zri Brettler (Oxford: Oxford University Press, 2004), 2041–47. I'm grateful to Robert Gagnon for pointing me to Klawans's work.

[5] It's important to note from this passage that the Old Testament penalties of death or banishment for egregious sexual sin are now realized in the church through excommunication. "Purge the evil person from among you" (1 Cor. 5:13), which Paul uses to refer to excommunication, is borrowed from the death penalty texts of Deuteronomy (e.g., 17:7; 19:19).

eating shellfish.[6] Leviticus was part of the Bible Jesus read, the Bible Jesus believed, and the Bible Jesus did not want to abolish. We ought to take seriously how the Holiness Code reveals to us the holy character of God and the holy people we are supposed to be. Even on this side of the cross the commands in Leviticus still matter. When the Gentiles entered the church centuries later, they did not have to become Jews (1 Cor. 7:19), but in keeping with God's moral law, they did have to leave sexual immorality behind (5:11; 6:18; 10:8).

---

[6] See, for example, the helpful post from Tim Keller, "Making Sense of Scripture's 'Inconsistency,'" The Gospel Coalition, July 9, 2012, http://www.thegospelcoalition.org/article/making -sense-of-scriptures-inconsistency.

4

The Romans Road in the Wrong Direction

ROMANS 1

The most detailed and significant treatment of homosexuality is found in the first chapter of the most important letter in the history of the world. Romans 1 reinforces with unambiguous clarity all that we've seen up to this point from the Old Testament; namely, that homosexual practice is a serious sin and a violation of God's created order.

Let's try to break down Paul's argument in Romans 1:18–32 and understand why he concludes that same-sex sexual activity, like idolatry, is an affront to the design of the Creator.

Wrath Revealed (vv. 18–20)

For the wrath of God is revealed from heaven against all ungodliness and unrighteousness of men, who by their unrighteousness suppress the truth. For what can be known about God is plain to them, because God has shown it to them. For his invisible attributes, namely, his eternal power and divine nature, have been clearly perceived, ever since the creation of the world, in the things that have been made. So they are without excuse.

The argument of Romans 1 is held together by the interplay of two revelations. The righteousness of God is revealed through the saving message of the gospel (vv. 16–17), while the wrath of God is revealed through God's punishment of ungodliness and unrighteousness (v. 18). Both revelations depend upon knowledge. We cannot be saved by faith apart from knowledge of the gospel (cf. 10:14–15), while conversely, we would not be judged except that we have some knowledge of God through the created world (1:19–20). God is always fair. He does not condemn the innocent and the ignorant.

And yet, verses 19 and 20 inform us that none are innocent because none are wholly ignorant (cf. 3:10–18, 23). From the natural world and from the law written on our own hearts, we know the truth about God, or at least enough of the truth to leave us without excuse (Ps. 19:1–6; Eccl. 3:11; Rom. 2:14–15). The wrath of God *is* revealed—in the handing over to greater iniquity (Rom. 1:24, 26, 28)—and *will be* revealed on the day of judgment (2:5) because the peoples of the world suppress the truth about God and do not worship him as he desires and as he deserves.

Having explained the predicament of the fallen world (specifically the Gentile world), Paul then explains in more detail how the truth about God has been suppressed in unrighteousness. Rampant human depravity can be seen in three exchanges.

First Exchange (vv. 21–23)

For although they knew God, they did not honor him as God or give thanks to him, but they became futile in their thinking, and their foolish hearts were darkened. Claiming to be wise, they became fools, and exchanged the glory of the immortal God for images resembling mortal man and birds and animals and creeping things.

First, we see the ungodliness of men in exchanging the glory of the immortal God for the foolishness of idolatry (v. 23). Instead of giving thanks to the God of heaven, the nations of the world worship images resembling human beings, birds, animals, and creeping things (and our sometimes less visible, but not less insidious, idols of power, money, and approval are no better). Such darkness comes from futile thinking and a foolish heart (Isa. 44:9–20).

Second Exchange (vv. 24–25)

Therefore God gave them up in the lusts of their hearts to impurity, to the dishonoring of their bodies among themselves, because they exchanged the truth about God for a lie and worshiped and served the creature rather than the Creator, who is blessed forever! Amen.

Second, we see the ungodliness of men in exchanging the truth about God for a lie. The pagan peoples of the world have served the creature instead of worshiping the Creator. Importantly, the transition from the first to the second exchange is marked by God "[giving] them up in the lusts of their hearts to impurity" (v. 24). We see this after each exchange: God progressively handing sinners over to more and more ungodliness. In this step of the process God gives them up to uncleanness (*akatharsia*), a word in the New Testament almost always associated with immorality, especially sexual immorality. That Paul is not thinking of mere ritual uncleanness is clear from the way in which he uses *akatharsia* in his writings (Rom. 6:19;

2 Cor. 12:21; Gal. 5:19; Eph. 4:19; 5:3; Col. 3:5; 1 Thess. 2:3; 4:7) and by the reference to "dishonoring of their bodies" in the second half of verse 24.

Third Exchange (vv. 26–27)

> For this reason God gave them up to dishonorable passions. For their women exchanged natural relations for those that are contrary to nature; and the men likewise gave up natural relations with women and were consumed with passion for one another, men committing shameless acts with men and receiving in themselves the due penalty for their error.

The next step in the progression of sin is God handing the Gentiles over to dishonorable passions. This leads to the third exchange: giving up natural relations with members of the opposite sex for relations with those of the same sex. Paul's burden is not to rank the relative heinousness of homosexual sin. Although he would have embraced the Old Testament distinction between unintentional sins and high-handed sins (Num. 15:27–31), his point is more illustrative than evaluative. In Paul's mind, same-sex sexual intimacy is an especially clear illustration of the idolatrous human impulse to turn away from God's order and design. Those who suppress the truth about God as revealed in nature suppress the truth about themselves written in nature. Homosexual practice is an example on a horizontal plane of our vertical rebellion against God.

The emphasis on exchange makes clear that Paul is thinking of homosexual activity in general and not just a "bad" kind of homosexuality. The issue cannot be pederasty because there is no record of adult-youth sexual intimacy among women in the ancient world. Likewise, the issue cannot be master-slave relationships or other sexual abuse more generically because Paul speaks of both parties being "consumed with passion for one another" (v. 27). Gender is the point, not orientation or exploitation or domination. The issue is exchanging the natural relationship between a man and a woman for unnatural same-sex relationships.

Revisionist authors sometimes argue that excess was the real problem. The ungodly in Paul's mind were those who, though capable of heterosexual attraction, became dissatisfied with their usual sexual activity, lusted after new experiences, and sought out homosexual encounters. No doubt, much of homosexual practice in the ancient world was by men who also had sex with women, but this does not mean Paul had no concept of orientation or that the category would have altered his final conclusion. Even if Paul did not use our modern vocabulary, his judgment is still the same. Homosexual behavior is a sin, not according to who practices it or by what motivation they seek it, but because that act itself, as a truth-suppressing exchange, is contrary to God's good design. Every passion directed toward illegitimate ends was considered excessive and lacking in self-control (Titus 1:12). The word for natural "relations" (*kresis*) in Romans 1:27 does not speak to the state of our desires, but to the state of our design, which is why the KJV has "natural use" and the NASB has "natural function."[1] The problem with the consuming passion in verse 27 was not its intensity but that it corresponded to the giving up of man's natural sexual complementarity with women and committing shameless acts with other men.

The phrase "contrary to nature" translates the Greek words *para physin*. The phrase was commonly used in the ancient world to speak of deviant forms of sexual activity, especially homosexual behavior. We find examples of *para physin* being used as a reference to homosexual practice in writers as diverse

---

[1] Greg Koukl, "Paul, Romans, and Homosexuality," Stand to Reason, February 4, 2013, http://www.str.org/articles/paul-romans-and-homosexuality#.VMZz8v7F-Dl/.

as Plato, Plutarch, Philo, and Josephus.[2] Stoic philosophers employ the phrase "contrary to nature" to the same effect. For example, Musonius Rufus, a popular philosopher who lived around the same time as the Apostle Paul, observed, "But of all sexual relations those involving adultery are most unlawful, and no more tolerable are those of men with men, because it is a monstrous thing and contrary to nature."[3] Even when Paul references nature (*physis*) in 1 Corinthians 11:14—a more difficult passage for the conservative to explain since it has to do with hair length and hairstyle—the meaning (if not the application) is nevertheless plain: there is a divine design to manhood and womanhood that should not be transgressed. The use of the phrase in Romans 11:24, where Paul says the Gentiles were grafted into the people of God "contrary to nature" (*para physin*), is somewhat different, but still connotes divine order and design.

In the end, however, we don't need detailed word studies from the writings of Greeks and Romans and Hellenistic Jews to tell us what Paul is talking about. The context gives us all the clues we need. Not only do we have the language of exchange; we have obvious allusions to the Genesis creation account:

- The creation of the world is mentioned in verse 20.
- The Creator is mentioned in verse 25.
- The language of animals, birds, and creeping things in verse 23 echoes Genesis 1:30.
- The Greek in verse 23 mirrors the Septuagint (Greek) version of Genesis 1:26, with both passages using iden-

---

[2] See Thomas E. Schmidt, *Straight and Narrow? Compassion and Clarity in the Homosexuality Debate* (Downers Grove, IL: InterVarsity Press, 1995), 79–80; Richard B. Hays, *The Moral Vision of the New Testament: A Contemporary Introduction to New Testament Ethics* (New York: Harper One, 1996), 387–89.

[3] Thomas K. Hubbard, ed., *Homosexuality in Greece and Rome: A Sourcebook of Basic Documents* (Berkeley, CA: University of California Press, 2003), 394–95. Stoic philosophy was opposed to any form of sex that was considered unnatural (ibid., 10, 385).

tical words for *image, likeness, man, birds, four-footed animals*, and *creeping things*.

- The language of a lie (v. 25), and shame (v. 27), and the sentence of death (v. 32) are allusions to the fall in Genesis 3.[4]

With these allusions to creation in the background (the foreground really), "nature" must mean more than "prevailing customs and social norms." When Paul faults homosexual behavior for being contrary to nature, it's not like condemning deaf persons for speaking with their hands in an "unnatural" way. That may seem like a good analogy, but it's one Paul never makes, because it's one about which the creation account does not speak. By contrast, Genesis has much to say about the nature of male-female complementarity. Homosexual practice is sinful because it violates the divine design in creation. According to Paul's logic, men and women who engage in same-sex sexual behavior—even if they are being true to their own feelings and desires—have suppressed God's truth in unrighteousness. They have exchanged the fittedness of male-female relations for those that are contrary to nature.

Death Deserved (vv. 28–32)

And since they did not see fit to acknowledge God, God gave them up to a debased mind to do what ought not to be done. They were filled with all manner of unrighteousness, evil, covetousness, malice. They are full of envy, murder, strife, deceit, maliciousness. They are gossips, slanderers, haters of God, insolent, haughty, boastful, inventors of evil, disobedient to parents, foolish, faithless, heartless, ruthless. Though they know God's righteous decree that those who

---

[4] For more detail on these connections, see Robert A. J. Gagnon, *The Bible and Homosexual Practice: Texts and Hermeneutics* (Nashville, TN: Abingdon, 2001), 289–93.

practice such things deserve to die, they not only do them but give approval to those who practice them.

Following the third exchange, we have one final handing over—"God gave them up to a debased mind." This debased mind produces a host of unrighteous thoughts, attitudes, and actions, the sentence for which is death. In one sense, we should not make too much of homosexual sin, given the long list of sins mentioned in verses 29–31. And yet the fact that Paul singles out homosexual relations as a conspicuous example of the human heart suppressing the truth and turning from God suggests that we must not soft-pedal as no big deal what the Bible underlines as particularly egregious rebellion. And it means we must face squarely the serious indictment God's Word levies against the individuals and churches that "give approval to those who practice them" (v. 32). It is no little mistake in God's eyes to encourage and support what harms our fellow creatures and dishonors our Creator.

It also needs to be stated that the turn of the page to Romans 2 does not negate everything that was said in Romans 1. No doubt, Paul is springing something of a trap for his Jewish readers. As soon as his kinsmen according to the flesh start getting comfortable in condemning the vile sins of the Gentiles, Paul turns the tables on them: "Therefore you have no excuse, O man, every one of you who judges. For in passing judgment on another you condemn yourself, because you, the judge, practice the very same things" (2:1). Paul is not claiming that everyone is guilty of every sin mentioned in Romans 1 or even in verses 28–32. His point, rather, is that everyone is guilty of these sorts of sins and in need of a Savior. No one is righteous, all have sinned and fallen short of the glory of God— that's the conclusion toward which Paul is pressing (3:10–26). Just because Paul wants us to see our own sin does not mean that all moral iniquity ceases to be sin. Even on the other side of the trap in Romans 2 we see the indispensability of personal holiness (6:1–23; 12:1–2) and the darkness of sexual immorality (13:11–14). The impurity (*akatharsia*) exposed in Romans 1:24 is the impurity (*akatharsia*) in Romans 6:19 to which we must not present our members (i.e., sexual organs) as slaves and from which we must flee.

Final Thought

There is no way to "rescue" Paul from his strong condemnation of homosexual behavior. We can't make "unclean" mean "ritually impure." We can't make "contrary to nature" mean "out of the ordinary" or "against my personal orientation." We can't make this text about nothing more than pederasty, exploitation, and excess passion. The allusions to Genesis and the emphasis on the "exchange" present in same-sex sexual intimacy will not allow for any other conclusion but the traditional one: God's people ought not engage in homosexual behavior or give approval to those who do (1:32).

5

A New Word from an Old Place

1 CORINTHIANS 6; 1 TIMOTHY 1

The vast majority of people reading this chapter have never formally studied Koine Greek, the language of the New Testament. And yet, this whole chapter is about the meaning of two Greek words. That makes this a daunting chapter, both for you to read and for me to write. But hopefully with some careful thinking and a little common sense you'll find that the matter does not have to be as complicated as some make it out to be.

I'll start by introducing the two Greek words. Then I'll make a few points about how to define debatable words. And after all that we'll get down to the business of trying to figure out what these two words mean.

Two Debatable Words

The two words in question, *malakoi* and *arsenokoitai*, can be found in two different places in the New Testament. Here's how the verses read in the English Standard Version:

Or do you not know that the unrighteous will not inherit the kingdom of God? Do not be deceived: neither the sexually immoral, nor idolaters, nor adulterers, nor men who practice homosexuality [*oute malakoi oute arsenokoitai*], nor thieves, nor the greedy, nor drunkards, nor revilers, nor swindlers will inherit the kingdom of God. (1 Cor. 6:9–10)

Now we know that the law is good, if one uses it lawfully, understanding this, that the law is not laid down for the just but for the lawless and disobedient, for the ungodly and sinners, for the unholy and profane, for those who strike their fathers and mothers, for murderers, the sexually immoral, men who practice homosexuality [*arsenokoitai*], enslavers, liars, perjurers, and whatever else is contrary to sound doctrine, in accordance with the gospel of the glory of the blessed God with which I have been entrusted. (1 Tim. 1:8–11)

Other popular translations look similar, except whereas the ESV combines *malakoi* and *arsenokoitai* into one phrase ("men who practice homosexuality"), most English Bibles (though not all) render the two words separately. Figure 5.1 shows how the major English translations handle *malakoi . . . arsenokoitai* in 1 Corinthians 6:19 and *arsenokoitai* in 1 Timothy 1:10.

With the exception of the four-centuries-old King James Version, which describes the sin in euphemistic terms ("abusers of themselves with mankind"), all the modern versions explicitly link *arsenokoitai* to homosexual behavior (which is what the KJV was getting at, too). The other word in question, *malakoi*, is not treated as uniformly, but just from looking at the major English translations we can see it is some kind of sin related to homosexuality. We'll come back to both words in a moment.

Figure 5.1

	malakoi ... arseno-koitai (1 Cor. 6:9)	arsenokoitai (1 Tim. 1:10)
English Standard Version	men who practice homosexuality	men who practice homosexuality
Holman Christian Standard Bible	anyone practicing homosexuality	homosexuals
King James Version	effeminate ... abusers of themselves with mankind	them that defile themselves with mankind
New American Bible	boy prostitutes ... practicing homosexuals	practicing homo-sexuals
New American Standard Bible	effeminate ... homosexuals	homosexuals
New International Version (2011)	men who have sex with men	those practicing homosexuality
New King James Version	homosexuals ... sodomites	sodomites
New Living Translation	male prostitutes ... [those who] practice homo-sexuality	[those who] practice homo-sexuality
New Revised Standard Version	male prostitutes, sodomites	sodomites

How to Define Difficult Words

As you might have guessed, not everyone agrees on how best to translate *malakoi* and *arsenokoitai*. Revisionist authors argue that the words mean something other than men having sex with men. Some say these words should be understood narrowly, referring only to a specific kind of homosexual behavior, like pederasty or prostitution. Others claim that the words are quite broad and refer to any man in the ancient world who seemed unduly feminine or passive or controlled by his passions. In either case, the revisionist argument amounts to the same thing: the condemnations in 1 Corinthians 6:9 and 1 Timothy 1:10 are not talking about committed, consensual same-sex relationships as we know them today.

Before wading through the weeds of *malakoi* and *arsenokoitai*, it may be helpful to think through a few issues related to the definition of biblical words.

(1) The English translations are almost always right, especially when they basically say the same thing. Think about it: each of the nine translations listed above was put together by a team of scholars with expertise in biblical scholarship and the original languages. That doesn't mean they can't make mistakes or that we can't learn new things they missed. But it does mean that after reading a few commentaries and perusing a couple articles online you will certainly not know the ancient world or Koine Greek better than they did. If the translators thought a specific word *really* meant X (as seminary students and bloggers are apt to say), they wouldn't have translated it as Y. Our English translations, imperfect though they may be, are faithful and reliable translations of the original languages. They do not need decoding.

(2) Words have a semantic range of meaning. This is a fancy way of saying words don't always mean exactly the same thing. You can run *fast*, then put the food away and start a *fast*, just as long as you don't play *fast* and loose with me. So what does *fast* mean? That depends. Or to use an example from the Bible, think about the word *world*. It can refer to the fallen ways of mankind that we should not love (1 John 2:15–17) or the fallen race of mankind that God so loved (John 3:16). In determining what specific words mean in the Bible it can be helpful to see

how the same word is used in another Greek text. But we need to be careful. The examples we find are often by different authors writing from different places living in different centuries. Seeing how a disputed word was used in the ancient world gets us in the definitional ballpark but rarely will word studies be decisive, especially the further out from the text we have to go. So how do we know what words mean?

(3) Context is king. The most important step in defining difficult words is to see how they are used in the flow of the text. What are the other words around it? What argument is the author trying to make? How does he use the word elsewhere in the same writing? Is the word used in another text by the same author? Lexical meaning is best determined by looking at concentric circles that start small and move outward. Plato, a Greek philosopher four hundred years before Paul, is not as relevant to understanding Paul as Philo, a Jewish philosopher roughly contemporary with Paul. And digging into Philo's work is not nearly as critical as understanding Paul's background, examining Paul's sentences, and tracing Paul's arguments.

Getting Down to Business

So what do these two disputed words mean? Let's look at *arsenokoitai* first and then *malakoi*.

There are no examples of *arsenokoitai* in the surviving Greek literature prior to Paul's use of the term in 1 Corinthians and 1 Timothy. The word is a compound of man (*arsēn*) and bed (*koitē*) and could literally be translated "bedders of men" or "those who take males to bed." Most likely, Paul coined the term from the prohibitions against homosexual behavior in Leviticus 18 and 20. Remember Paul's background: he was a Jew, of the tribe of Benjamin, mentored by the famed Gamaliel, and educated according to the strictest manner of the law of his fathers (Acts 22:3; cf. Phil. 3:5–6). He knew the Scripture far better than he knew any other writings. If Shakespeare's plays are steeped in biblical allusions and biblical imagery, how much more should we expect to find careful references to the Old Testament in Paul—an impeccably trained Pharisee and the preeminent theologian of the early church.

You don't have to be an expert in Greek to see how Paul got the word *arsenokoitai* from Leviticus. Here's what the relevant texts look like in the Septuagint (the Greek translation of the Old Testament used by Jews in the first century):

Leviticus 18:22 *meta **arsenos** ou koimēthēsē **koitēn** gynaikos* ("you shall not lie with a male as with a woman")

Leviticus 20:13 *hos an koimēthē meta **arsenos** **koitēn** gynaikos* ("whoever shall lie with a male as with a woman")

You can see from the second text in particular how Paul's use of *arsenokoitai* is almost certainly taken from the Holiness Code of Leviticus. It's clear from 1 Timothy 1:9–10 that Paul, in speaking of *arsenokoitai*, was thinking broadly about the sins forbidden by the Decalogue: "those who strike their fathers and mothers" (fifth commandment), "murderers" (sixth commandment), "the sexually immoral, men who practice homosexuality" (seventh commandment), "enslavers" (eighth commandment), "liars, perjurers" (ninth commandment). No Jew thought the Ten Commandments allowed for same-sex sexual intimacy, so no one would have been surprised to see homosexual behavior—or adultery or fornication or prostitution or incest or bestiality or any other sexual activity outside of marriage—thrown into a vice list by the Apostle Paul.

If he wanted to shock Timothy and upset his fellow Jews and blow up the prevailing ethos in the early church by allowing for committed same-sex relationships, Paul picked an impossibly obscure way of introducing such a radical change. Why not use the word *paiderastes* (pederasts, adult males who have sex with boys) if that's all Paul had in mind? Likewise, if Paul wanted his readers to know he was referring only to exploitative forms of homosexuality, he wouldn't have coined a term from a portion of the Mosaic law where all sex involving a man with a man is forbidden. Was Paul opposed only to exploitative forms of incest in 1 Corinthians 5? Was he telling those Christians entangled in sexual immorality to flee only from exploitative forms of adultery, fornication, and prostitution in the second half of 1 Corinthians 6? Are we really to suppose that Paul—just after urging excommunication for sexual sin (5:4–5, 13), and just as he references the Mosaic law (6:9), and just before he anchors his sexual ethic in the Genesis creation story (6:16)—meant to say, "Obviously, I'm not talking about two adult men in a long-term relationship"? And if he had meant to communicate such a message to the Corinthians or to Timothy, how would that have been obvious to any of them?

From the etymology of the word and from its roots in Leviticus, we can be confident that *arsenokoitai* carries the basic meaning: "men who have sex with other men." "Sodomites" is not the best translation because there is nothing in 1 Corinthians or 1 Timothy which links *arsenokoitai* with the story of Sodom and Gomorrah. Likewise, "homosexuals" does not make sufficiently clear whether we are talking about everyone who experiences same-sex attraction or those who self-identify as gay or something else. The best translations communicate the notion of activity; *arsenokoitai* refers to men engaged in homosexual behavior. It's the shameless act Paul describes in Romans 1:27 as being committed *arsenes en arsesin* ("men in men").[1]

---

[1] The phrase *arsenes en arsesin* could also be translated using the preposition "with," but "men *in* men"—which is how the Latin Vulgate renders the Greek (*masculi in masculos*)—is likely an explicit, if somewhat graphic, reference to the homosexual act itself.

This is why early translations of the New Testament translate *arsenokoitai* as "men lying together with males" (Latin), "those who lie with men" (Syriac), and "lying with males" (Coptic).[2]

And what about the other disputed word? The standard Greek lexicon of the New Testament lists two definitions for *malakōs* (singular of *malakoi*): "being yielding to touch" and "being passive in a same-sex relationship."[3] The word can mean soft, as in soft clothing (Matt. 11:8; Luke 7:25), or effeminate, as in men who are penetrated (like a female would be) by another man.

Could Paul be using the word more broadly to refer to men who had made themselves overly feminine in appearance or demeanor? It's possible that's part of what Paul means by *malakoi*, but it's unlikely that's all Paul means. Paul thought it was a disgrace for men to have hair like women (1 Cor. 11:14), but he never suggests that hairstyles jeopardize one's eternal standing before God. It would be strange to think—and unpalatable to most Christians on the revisionist side—that Paul was excluding from the kingdom of God men with a hankering for fine clothes and romantic comedies; *malakoi* must refer to something more serious.

The vice list in 1 Corinthians 6 is specifically tailored for the Corinthians. There are a series of vices related to the church's problems with sexual sin in chapters 5 and 6 ("neither the sexually immoral, nor idolaters [which may include notions of sexual sin[4]], nor adulterers, nor *malakoi*, nor *arsenokoitai*" [6:9]), and then five more sins related to the church's prob-

---

[2] As quoted in Robert A. J. Gagnon, *The Bible and Homosexual Practice: Texts and Hermeneutics* (Nashville, TN: Abingdon, 2001), 322.

[3] *A Greek-English Lexicon of the New Testament and Other Early Christian Literature, Third Edition*, rev. and ed. Frederick William Danker, based on Walter Bauer's lexicon (Chicago: University of Chicago Press, 2000).

[4] See, for example, from the Apocrypha, the Wisdom of Solomon: "For the idea of making idols was the beginning of fornication, and the invention of them was the corruption of life" (14:12). See also Rev. 2:14, 20.

lems with the Lord's Supper in chapter 11 ("nor thieves, nor the greedy, nor drunkards, nor revilers, nor swindlers" [6:10]). Sandwiched between adulterers (*moichoi*) and men who practice homosexuality (*arsenokoitai*), *malakoi* must refer to some kind of immoral sexual intimacy, not just an effeminate pattern in speech, deportment, or passions.

This understanding of *malakoi* and *arsenokoitai* (as outlined above) fits with the consensus of modern English translations, fits with the ethics of the Old Testament, fits with the training Paul would have received as a Jewish scholar, and, most importantly, fits within the context of Paul's argument. It's as if in 1 Corinthians 6 Paul is saying, "Do not be deceived: the sexually immoral will not inherit the kingdom of God, and this includes those who have sex as a part of a pagan ritual, those who have sex with someone other than their spouse, men who play the passive role in homosexual activity, and—in keeping with the general prohibition found in the Torah—any male who has sex with another male." The disputed words are not so broad as to include feminized heterosexual behavior or so narrow as to exclude everything but exploitative homosexual behavior. Both terms refer to men who have sex with other men, the passive and the active partners. Paul is saying what we find hard to hear but what the rest of the Bible supports and most of church history has assumed: homosexual activity is not a blessing to be celebrated and solemnized but a sin to be repented of, forsaken, and forgiven.

Part 2

ANSWERING OBJECTIONS

6

"The Bible Hardly Ever Mentions Homosexuality"

The first step in delegitimizing what the Bible says about homosexuality is to suggest that the Bible hardly says anything about homosexuality. As I mentioned in the introduction, in one sense this is true. The Bible is a big book, and the rightness or wrongness of homosexual practice is not at the center of it. If you read through the 1,189 chapters in the Bible and the more than 30,000 verses, you'll find only a dozen or so passages that deal explicitly with homosexuality. We looked at most of them in part 1 of this book.

So does this mean the traditional view of marriage is based on nothing more than a few fragments? Is it fair to say that just six or seven passages have for centuries prevented those engaged in homosexual activity from finding acceptance in the church? Are denominations and families and friendships and organizations and institutions being torn apart because of a small handful of disputed texts concerning a minor issue about which Jesus never even said anything? Or to ask the question another way: if the Bible says so little about homosexuality, why do Christians insist on talking about it so much?

A Fair Question with Plenty of Answers

Let me make six points by way of response.

(1) We need to remember that this controversy was not dreamed up by evangelical Christians. If traditionalists are writing blogs and books by the dozens, it's because revisionist leaders first wanted to have the conversation. The reason there is so much discussion about issues like abortion, euthanasia, and same-sex marriage is because many have sought to legalize and legitimize actions that were until fifty years ago considered immoral and illegal. When it comes to the cultural flash points of our day, it hardly seems wise to avoid talking about what everyone else is talking about.

(2) The reason the Bible says comparatively little about homosexuality is because it was a comparatively uncontroversial sin among ancient Jews and Christians. There is no evidence that ancient Judaism or early Christianity tolerated any expression of homosexual activity. The Bible says a lot about idolatry, religious hypocrisy, economic injustice, and pagan worship because these were common sins for God's people in both testaments. The prophets didn't rail against homosexual practice because as a particularly obvious and egregious sin it was less frequently committed in the covenant community. The Bible talks about bestiality even less than it talks about homosexuality, but that doesn't make bestiality an insignificant issue—or incest or child abuse or fifty other sins the Bible barely addresses. Counting up the number of verses on any particular topic is not the best way to determine the seriousness of the sin involved.

(3) Having said all that, it's not like the Bible is silent on the

issue of homosexual behavior. It's explicitly condemned in the Mosaic law (Leviticus) and used as a vivid example of human rebellion in Paul's most important letter (Romans). It's listed among a host of other serious vices in two different epistles (1 Corinthians and 1 Timothy). It's one of the reasons God destroyed the most infamous cities in the Bible (Sodom and Gomorrah). And that's not even mentioning all the texts about marriage in Genesis, in Proverbs, in Song of Solomon, in Malachi, in Matthew, and in Ephesians. When the Bible speaks in a single verse—as an aside, with no agreed upon historical interpretation—about people being baptized on behalf of the dead (1 Cor. 15:29), we are right to think this is not a matter that should detain us long and one we should not be too dogmatic about. The biblical witness concerning homosexual behavior is not at all this obscure or this isolated.[1]

(4) Furthermore, there is nothing ambiguous about the biblical witness concerning homosexual behavior. Even many revisionist scholars acknowledge that the Bible is uniformly negative toward same-sex activity. The gay Dutch scholar Pim Pronk, after admitting that many Christians are eager to see homosexuality supported by the Bible, states plainly, "In this case that support is lacking."[2] Although he doesn't think moral positions must be dependent on the Bible (which is why he can support homosexual behavior), as a scholar he recognizes that "wherever homosexual intercourse is mentioned in Scripture, it is condemned. . . . Rejection is a foregone conclusion; the

---

[1] How many verses in the Bible speak directly to the issue of homosexuality? Robert Gagnon provides the following list: Gen. 9:20–27; 19:4–11; Lev. 18:22; 20:13; Judg. 19:22–25; Ezek. 16:50 (possibly 18:12 and 33:26); Rom. 1:26–27; 1 Cor. 6:9; 1 Tim. 1:10; and probably 2 Pet. 2:7 and Jude 7. Texts referring to homosexual cult prostitution could also be added: Deut. 23:17–18; 1 Kings 14:24; 15:12; 22:46; 2 Kings 23:7; Job 36:14; and possibly Rev. 21:8; 22:15. The Bible talks about homosexuality more than we might think (Robert A. J. Gagnon, *The Bible and Homosexual Practice: Texts and Hermeneutics* [Nashville, TN: Abingdon, 2001], 432).

[2] Pim Pronk, *Against Nature? Types of Moral Argumentation Regarding Homosexuality* (Grand Rapids, MI: Eerdmans, 1993), 323.

assessment of it nowhere constitutes a problem."[3] Pronk recognizes that wherever the Bible speaks on this issue, it speaks with one voice. Likewise, Dan O. Via, in arguing for the revisionist view opposite Robert Gagnon, acknowledges, "Professor Gagnon and I are in substantial agreement that the biblical texts that deal specifically with homosexual practice condemn it unconditionally."[4] No positive argument for homosexuality can be made from the Bible, only arguments that texts don't mean what they seem to mean, and that specific texts can be overridden by other considerations.

(5) It cannot be overstated how seriously the Bible treats the sin of sexual immorality. Sexual sin is never considered *adiaphora*, a matter of indifference, an agree-to-disagree issue like food laws or holy days (Rom. 14:1–15:7). To the contrary, sexual immorality is precisely the sort of sin that characterizes those who will not enter the kingdom of heaven. There are at least eight vice lists in the New Testament (Mark 7:21–22; Rom. 1:24–31; 13:13; 1 Cor. 6:9–10; Gal. 5:19–21; Col. 3:5–9; 1 Tim. 1:9–10; Rev. 21:8), and sexual immorality is included in *every* one of these. In fact, in seven of the eight lists there are multiple references to sexual immorality (e.g., impurity, sensuality, orgies, men who practice homosexuality), and in most of the passages some kind of sexual immorality heads the lists. You would be hard-pressed to find a sin more frequently, more uniformly, and more seriously condemned in the New Testament than sexual sin.

(6) To insist that Jesus never said anything about homosexuality is not really accurate. Not only did he explicitly reaffirm the creation account of marriage as the one-flesh union of a man and a woman (Matt. 19:4–6; Mark 10:6–9); he condemned the

---

[3] Ibid., 279.
[4] Dan O. Via and Robert Gagnon, *Homosexuality and the Bible: Two Views* (Minneapolis: Fortress Press, 2003), 93.

sin of *porneia* (Mark 7:21), a broad word encompassing every kind of sexual sin. The leading New Testament lexicon defines *porneia* as "unlawful sexual intercourse, prostitution, unchastity, fornication."[5] Likewise, New Testament scholar James Edwards states that *porneia* "can be found in Greek literature with reference to a variety of illicit sexual practices, including adultery, fornication, prostitution, and homosexuality. In the Old Testament it occurs for any sexual practice outside marriage between a man and a woman that is prohibited by the Torah."[6] Jesus didn't have to give a special sermon on homosexuality because all of his listeners understood that same-sex behavior was prohibited in the Pentateuch and reckoned as one of the many expressions of sexual sin (*porneia*) off limits for the Jews. Besides all this, there's no reason to treat Jesus's words (all of which were recorded by someone other than Jesus) as more authoritative than the rest of the Bible. He affirmed the abiding authority of the Old Testament (Matt. 5:17–18) and understood that his disciples would fill out the true meaning of his person and work (John 14:25–26; 16:12–15; cf. Luke 24:48–49; Acts 1:1–2).

A Third Way

When the Bible uniformly and unequivocally says the same thing about a serious sin, it seems unwise to find a third way which allows for some people to promote this sin. Of course, there could be a third way if the other two ways are "perform same-sex weddings" or "be an obnoxious jerk and shun those who disagree." No doubt, many on the traditional side must grow in asking questions, listening patiently, and demonstrating

---

[5] *A Greek-English Lexicon of the New Testament and Other Early Christian Literature, Third Edition,* rev. and ed. Frederick William Danker, based on Walter Bauer's lexicon (Chicago: University of Chicago Press, 2000), 854.
[6] James R. Edwards, *The Gospel According to Mark,* Pillar New Testament Commentary (Grand Rapids, MI: Eerdmans, 2001), 213.

Christlike love. But those advocating for a third way usually mean more than this. They want churches and denominations and institutions to come to an "agree to disagree" compromise. They want a moratorium on making definitive pronouncements until we've all had the chance to mull things over a good deal longer. With so many emotions and so many things to learn, shouldn't we keep talking to each other?

Talking is not the problem. The problem is when incessant talking becomes a cover for indecision or even cowardice. As one who has pastored for more than a dozen years in a mainline denomination, I have seen this far too often. It's death by dialogue. The conversation never stops after reaffirming the historic position. There will always be another paper, another symposium, and another round of conversation. The moratorium on making pronouncements will only be lifted once the revisionist position has won out. Every doctrine central to the Christian faith and precious to you as a Christian has been hotly debated and disputed. If the "conversation" about the resurrection or the Trinity or the two natures of Christ continued as long as smart people on both sides disagreed, we would have lost orthodoxy long ago.

All of these third ways end up the same way: a behavior the Bible does not accept is treated as acceptable. "Agree to disagree" sounds like a humble "meet you in the middle" compromise, but it is a subtle way of telling conservative Christians that homosexuality is not a make-or-break issue and we are wrong to make it so. No one would think of proposing a third way if the sin were racism or human trafficking. To countenance such a move would be a sign of moral bankruptcy. Faithfulness to the Word of God compels us to view sexual immorality with the same seriousness. Living an ungodly life is contrary to the sound teaching that defines the Christian (1 Tim. 1:8–11; Titus 1:16). Darkness must not be confused with light. Grace must not be confused with license. Unchecked sin must not be confused with the good news of justification apart from works of the law. Far from treating sexual deviance as a lesser ethical issue, the New Testament sees it as a matter for excommunication (1 Corinthians 5), separation (2 Cor. 6:12–20), and a temptation for perverse compromise (Jude 3–16).

We cannot count same-sex behavior as an indifferent matter. Of course, homosexuality isn't the only sin in the world, nor is it the most critical one to address in many church contexts. But if 1 Corinthians 6 is right, it's not an overstatement to say that solemnizing same-sex sexual behavior—like supporting any form of sexual immorality—runs the risk of leading people to hell. Scripture often warns us—and in the severest terms—against finding our sexual identity apart from Christ and against pursuing sexual practice inconsistent with being in Christ (whether that's homosexual sin, or, much more frequently, heterosexual sin). The same is not true when it comes to sorting out the millennium or deciding which instruments to use in worship. When we tolerate the doctrine which affirms homosexual behavior, we are tolerating a doctrine which leads people further from God. This is not the mission Jesus gave his disciples when he told them to teach the nations everything he commanded. The biblical teaching is consistent and unambiguous: homosexual activity is not God's will for his people. Silence in the face of such clarity is not prudence, and hesitation in light of such frequency is not patience. The Bible says more than enough about homosexual practice for us to say something too.

7

"Not That Kind of Homosexuality"

Let me be blunt: the Bible says nothing good about homosexual practice.

That may sound like a harsh conclusion, but it's not all that controversial. As we have seen, even some revisionist scholars admit that "wherever homosexual intercourse is mentioned in Scripture, it is condemned."[1] There is simply no positive case to be made from the Bible for homosexual behavior. Arguments in favor of same-sex unions do not rest on gay-affirming exegetical conclusions as much as they try to show that traditional interpretations of Scripture are unwarranted. That is to say, the only way revisionist arguments make sense is if they can show that there is an impassable distance between the world of the Bible and our world.

Of all the arguments in favor of same-sex behavior, the cultural distance argument is the most foundational and the most

---

[1] Pim Pronk, *Against Nature? Types of Moral Argumentation Regarding Homosexuality* (Grand Rapids, MI: Eerdmans, 1993), 279.

common (at least among those for whom biblical authority is still important). Although the Mosaic law and Paul's letter to the Romans and the vice lists of the New Testament speak resoundingly against same-sex behavior, these texts (it is said) were addressing a different kind of same-sex behavior. The ancient world had no concept of sexual orientation, no understanding of egalitarian, loving, committed, monogamous, covenantal same-sex unions. The issue was not gender (whether the lovers were male or female), but gender roles (whether a man was overly feminized and acting like a woman). The issue was not men having sex with men, but men having sex with boys. The issue was not consensual same-sex sexual intimacy, but gang rape, power imbalances, and systemic oppression. The revisionist case can take many forms, but central to most of them is the "not *that* kind of homosexuality!" argument. We can safely set aside the scriptural prohibitions against homosexual behavior because we are comparing apples and oranges: we are talking in our day about committed, consensual, lifelong partnerships, something the biblical authors in their day knew nothing about.

Despite its frequency and popularity, there are at least two major problems with this line of thinking.

Silence Is Not Always Golden

For starters, the cultural distance argument is an argument from silence. The Bible nowhere limits its rejection of homosexuality to exploitative or pederastic (man-boy) forms of same-sex sexual intimacy. Leviticus forbids a male lying with a male as with a woman (Lev. 18:22; 20:13). The text says nothing about temple prostitution, effeminate men, or sexual domination. The prohibition is against men doing with men what ought only to be done with women in the covenant of marriage. Similarly, the same-sex sin condemned in Romans 1 is not simply un-controllable passion or the insatiable male libido that desires men in addition to women. According to Paul, the fundamental problem with homosexual behavior is that men and women *exchange* sexual intercourse with the opposite sex for unnatural relations with persons of the same sex (Rom. 1:26–27; cf. vv. 22, 25). If the biblical authors meant to frown upon only certain kinds of homosexual arrangements, they wouldn't have condemned the same-sex act itself in such absolute terms.

Because the Bible never limits its rejection of homosexual behavior to pederasty or exploitation, those wanting to affirm homosexual behavior can only make an argument from silence. That's why you will often read in the revisionist literature that the biblical author was only thinking of man-boy love or that an exploitative relationship would have been assumed in the minds of the original audience. The argument usually goes like this:

- There were many bad examples of homosexual behavior in the ancient world.
- For example, here are ancient sources describing pederasty, master-slave encounters, and wild promiscuity.
- Therefore, when the Bible condemns same-sex sexual behavior, it had these bad examples in mind.

This reasoning can look impressive, especially when it comes at you with a half dozen quotations from ancient sources that most readers are not familiar with. But the last step in the sequence is an assumption more than an argument. How can we be sure Paul had these bad examples in mind? If he did, why didn't he use the Greek word for pederasty? Why didn't he warn masters against forcing themselves upon slaves? Why does the Bible talk about men lying with men and the exchange of what is natural for unnatural if it wasn't thinking about the created order and only had in mind predatory sex and promiscuous liasons? If the biblical authors expected us to know what they *really* had in mind—and no one figured this out for two millennia—it appears that they came up with a remarkably ineffective way of getting their point across.

What Do the Texts Say?

The second reason the distance argument fails is because it is an argument against the evidence. The line of reasoning traced above would be more compelling if it could be demonstrated that the *only* kinds of homosexuality known in the ancient world were based on pederasty, victimization, and exploitation. On the face of it, it's strange that progressive voices would want us to reach this conclusion; it would mean that committed, consensual, lifelong partnerships were completely unknown and untried in the ancient world. It seems demeaning to suggest that until very recently in the history of the world there were no examples of warm, loving, committed homosexual relationships. This is probably why one popular-level revisionist author in using the cultural distance argument to make a biblical case for same-sex relationships admits, "This isn't to say *no one* [in the Greco-Roman world] pursued only same-sex relationships, or that no same-sex unions were marked by long-term commitment and love."[2] But of course, once we recognize that the type of same-sex unions progressives want to bless today were in fact present in the ancient world, it's only special pleading which makes us think the biblical prohibitions couldn't be talking about *those* kinds of relationships.

As a pastor I can read Greek, but I'm no expert in Plato, Plutarch, or Aristides. Most people reading this book are not classics scholars either. Thankfully, almost all of the important

---

[2] Matthew Vines, *God and the Gay Christian: The Biblical Case in Support of Same-Sex Relationships* (New York: Convergent Books, 2014), 104; emphasis in original.

ancient texts on homosexuality are readily available in English. It doesn't make for fun reading, but anyone can explore the primary sources in *Homosexuality in Greece and Rome: A Sourcebook of Basic Documents.* This 558-page book is edited by the non-Christian classics professor Thomas K. Hubbard. What you'll find in the sourcebook is not surprising given the diversity and complexity of the ancient world: homosexual behavior was not reducible to any single pattern, and moral judgment did not fall into neat categories. There was no more consensus about homosexuality in ancient Greece and Rome than we see today.[3]

From a Christian point of view, there are plenty of examples of "bad" homosexuality in the ancient world, but there is also plenty of evidence to prove that homosexual activity was not restricted to man-boy pairs. Some homosexual lovers swore continued attraction well into their loved one's adulthood, and some same-sex lovers were lifelong companions.[4] By the first century AD, the Roman Empire was increasingly divided on the issue of homosexuality. As public displays of same-sex indulgence grew, so did the moral condemnation of homosexual behavior.[5] Every kind of homosexual relationship was known in the first century, from lesbianism, to orgiastic behavior, to gender-malleable "marriage," to lifelong same-sex companionship. Hubbard's summary of early imperial Rome is important:

> The coincidence of such severity on the part of moralistic writers with the flagrant and open display of every form of homosexual behavior by Nero and other practitioners indicates a culture in which attitude about this issue in-

---

[3] Thomas K. Hubbard, ed., *Homosexuality in Greece and Rome: A Sourcebook of Basic Documents* (Berkeley: University of California Press, 2003), 7–8.
[4] Ibid., 5–6.
[5] Ibid., 383.

creasingly defined one's ideological and moral position. In other words, homosexuality in this era may have ceased to be merely another practice of personal pleasure and began to be viewed as an essential and central category of personal identity, exclusive of and antithetical to heterosexual orientation.[6]

If the ancient world not only had a category for committed same-sex relationships but also some understanding of homosexual orientation (to use our phrase), there is no reason to think the New Testament's prohibitions against same-sex behavior were only for pederasty and exploitation.

Hubbard is not the only scholar to see the full range of homosexual expression in the ancient world. William Loader, who has written eight significant books on sexuality in Judaism and early Christianity and is himself a strong proponent of same-sex marriage, points to examples of same-sex adult partnerships in the ancient world.[7]

Even more telling, Bernadette Brooten, who has written the most important book on lesbianism in antiquity and is herself a lesbian, has criticized many of the revisionist arguments regarding exploitation, pederasty, and orientation. In criticizing the orientation argument, she writes:

> Paul could have believed that *tribades* [the active female partners in a female homosexual bond], the ancient *kinaidoi* [the passive male partners in a male homosexual bond] and other sexually unorthodox persons were born that way and yet still condemn them as unnatural and shameful. . . . I believe that Paul used the word "exchanged" to indicate that people knew the natural sexual order of the universe and left it behind. . . . I see Paul as condemning all forms

---

[6] Ibid., 386.
[7] William Loader, *The New Testament on Sexuality* (Grand Rapids, MI: Eerdmans: 2012), 84.

of homoeroticism as the unnatural acts of people who had turned away from God.[8]

Nascent ideas about orientation were not unknown in the Greco-Roman era. Consider, for example, Aristophanes's oration in Plato's *Symposium* (ca. 385–370 BC), a series of speeches on Love (*Eros*) given by famous men at a drinking party in 416 BC. At this party we meet Pausanias, who was a lover of the host Agathon—both grown men. Pausanias applauds the naturalness and longevity of same-sex love. In the fourth speech we meet the comic poet Aristophanes, who proposes a convoluted theory, including notions of genetic causation, about why some men and women are attracted to persons of the same sex. Even if the speech is meant to be satire, it only works as satire by playing off the positive view of homosexual practice common in antiquity.[9]

Suggesting that the only kinds of homosexual practice known in the ancient world were those we disapprove of today does not take into account all the evidence. Here, for example, is N. T. Wright's informed conclusion:

> As a classicist, I have to say that when I read Plato's *Symposium*, or when I read the accounts from the early Roman empire of the practice of homosexuality, then it seems to me they knew just as much about it as we do. In particular, a point which is often missed, they knew a great deal about what people today would regard as longer-term, reasonably stable relations between two people of the same gender. This is not a modern invention, it's already there in Plato.

---

[8] Bernadette Brooten, *Love between Women: Early Christian Responses to Female Homoeroticism* (Chicago: University of Chicago Press, 1996), 244, as quoted in Robert A. J. Gagnon, "How Bad Is Homosexual Practice according to Scripture and Does Scripture's Indictment Apply to Committed Homosexual Unions?" January 2007, www.robgagnon.net/HowBadIs HomosexualPractice.htm.
[9] Robert A. J. Gagnon, *The Bible and Homosexual Practice: Texts and Hermeneutics* (Nashville, TN: Abingdon, 2001), 350–54.

The idea that in Paul's day it was always a matter of exploitation of younger men by older men or whatever . . . of course there was plenty of that then, as there is today, but it was by no means the only thing. They knew about the whole range of options there.[10]

And then there is this admission from the late Louis Crompton, a gay man and pioneer in queer studies, in his massive book *Homosexuality and Civilization*:

Some interpreters, seeking to mitigate Paul's harshness, have read the passage [in Romans 1] as condemning not homosexuals generally but only heterosexual men and women who experimented with homosexuality. According to this interpretation, Paul's words were not directed at "bona fide" homosexuals in committed relationships. But such a reading, however well-intentioned, seems strained and unhistorical. Nowhere does Paul or any other Jewish writer of this period imply the least acceptance of same-sex relations under any circumstances. The idea that homosexuals might be redeemed by mutual devotion would have been wholly foreign to Paul or any Jew or early Christian.[11]

I know it is usually poor form to pile up block quotations from other authors, but in this case it proves a point. Scholars of all different stripes have said the same thing: the cultural distance argument will not work. There is nothing in the biblical text to suggest Paul or Moses or anyone else meant to limit the scriptural condemnation of homosexual behavior. Likewise, there is no good reason to think from the hundreds of homosexuality-related texts found in the Greco-Roman period that the blanket rejection of homosexual behavior found in the

---

[10] John L. Allen Jr., "Interview with Anglican Bishop N. T. Wright of Durham, England," *National Catholic Reporter*, May 21, 2004, http://www.nationalcatholicreporter.org/word/wright.htm. Ellipses in the original. I've corrected the typo "today" to "day."

[11] Louis Crompton, *Homosexuality and Civilization* (Cambridge, MA: Belknap Press, 2003), 114.

Bible can be redeemed by postulating an impassable cultural distance between our world and the ancient world. There is no positive case for homosexual practice in the Bible and no historical background that will allow us to set aside what has been the plain reading of Scripture for twenty centuries. The only way to think the Bible is talking about every other kind of homosexuality except the kind we want to affirm is to be less than honest with the texts or less than honest with ourselves.

8

"What about Gluttony and Divorce?"

Why do conservative Christians make such a fuss about homosexuality? Why not deal with our own besetting sins? If we really cared about obeying the Bible and pursuing holiness, we'd be much more concerned about all the ways we excuse more common transgressions like divorce and gluttony. Sometimes this line of reasoning is meant to shame ("Take the plank out of your own eye, you hypocrite"). Sometimes it's meant to point out supposed inconsistencies ("Get your own house in order and then we'll talk"). And other times it's meant to dial down the seriousness of the situation ("No one lives up to God's ideal so let's call off the inquisition"). No matter the desired effect, the logic can be undeniably powerful.

But the strength of the logic is much less than the impression it leaves. We need to get past bumper sticker reasoning and ask whether there is any substance on the other side of the slogan.

Before I criticize the "What about . . ." arguments, I need to state this as clearly as possible: the church should not overlook its other sins just to make homosexual sin seem worse. Whether it's gluttony or divorce or greed or gossip or judgmentalism, we need to own up to our failings wherever and whenever we're sinning. While working on this book, I was preaching through the Sermon on the Mount, so week after week I had to come to grips, and help the congregation come to grips, with Jesus's challenging words on everything from anger to lust to revenge to bitterness to materialism to worry. In many instances, the first response to the "What about . . ." argument will often be, "You're right. That's a real problem. I need to examine my heart on that issue, and the church needs to take its 'respectable sins' more seriously."[1]

Their God Is Their Belly

With that necessary introduction in place (not out of the way, but in our hearts), let's look more closely at the arguments related to gluttony. I've read articles which raise the question, quite seriously, "Why are we asking whether those engaged in homosexual behavior will be in heaven when we should be asking if there will be fat people in heaven?" "Everyone's a biblical literalist until you bring up gluttony," is one clever line I've come across. I've seen critics of traditional marriage cite the statistic that the Bible contains three times as many exhortations against gluttony as against homosexuality. Sounds like we've gotten our priorities all out of whack.

But even if this statistic is true, do we really want to suggest that one sin is no big deal because we've been lax about a different sin? If Christians are wrongly tolerant of unrepentant gluttony, this is a matter of extreme importance. Sin separates us from God. When we choose to embrace it, celebrate it, and

---

[1] See Jerry Bridges, *Respectable Sins: Confronting the Sins We Tolerate* (Colorado Springs, CO: NavPress, 2007).

not repent of it, we keep ourselves away from God and away from heaven.

Gluttony is a favorite vice to throw into the rhetorical mix because it is one of the so-called Seven Deadly Sins and it seems like one we all commit. The earliest formation of the list of seven comes from Evagrius of Pontus, a desert monk and follower of Origen.[2] It's not surprising that an ascetic who lived in a commune separated from the world might consider the temptation for food one of his chief maladies. One can detect more than a little monkish asceticism and some Stoic disdain for the body in the Fathers' abhorrence of gluttony.

Throughout church history, theologians have understood the sin of gluttony in different ways. For some, immoderate desire is the real fault. For others, eating more than we need is the issue. According to Augustine, food itself is not the problem but rather how we seek it, for what reason, and to what effect. The Catholic catechism does not call them seven "deadly sins," but "capital sins," because they engender other sins and other vices.[3]

C. S. Lewis, with typical insight, has the demon Screwtape note how persnickety old ladies—the kind who always turn aside whatever is offered and always insist on a tiny cup of tea—can be just as guilty of gluttony by putting their wishes first, no matter how troublesome they may be to others. Health-conscious foodies beware: the problem of gluttony, according to Lewis, was not too much food, but too much attention to food. We might say, in the broadest ethical sense, that gluttony is using food in a way that dulls us from the spiritual and distracts us from God. That's certainly a danger for most of us, but it's not the same as enjoying a meal, feeling stuffed, or being overweight.

---

[2] See William H. Willimon, *Sinning Like a Christian: A New Look at the 7 Deadly Sins* (Nashville, TN: Abingdon Press, 2013), 3.
[3] *Catechism of the Catholic Church*, 1866.

And what does the Bible say? Some will be surprised to learn that *gluttony* appears in none of the New Testament vice lists. In fact, most of the Bible is overwhelmingly positive about food. There were plenty of feasts in the Old Testament and visions of heavenly feasts yet to come. Jesus finished his ministry with a meal and instituted a supper in remembrance of his death. If the New Testament has an overriding concern with food, it is that God's people not be overly concerned about it. Food does not commend us to God (1 Cor. 8:8), and the kingdom of God does not consist of food and drink (Rom. 14:17). No honest reader of the New Testament can deny that Jesus and the apostles were much more concerned about what we do sexually with our bodies than with the food we eat (Mark 7:21–23; 1 Cor. 6:12–20; cf. 1 Tim. 4:1–5).

In the English Standard Version, the word *glutton* appears four times and in every instance is paired with the word *drunkard* (Deut. 21:20; Prov. 23:21) or in a slander against Jesus (Matt. 11:19; Luke 7:34). The word *gluttonous* shows up once, again alongside a reference to *drunkards* (Prov. 23:20). Two other times we have *gluttons,* once in a quotation from a poet speaking of lazy Cretans (Titus 1:12) and the other time in reference to the company a shameful son keeps (Prov. 28:7).

The other passages often associated with gluttony are much less than meets the eye. For example, the point of Proverbs 23:2 ("put a knife to your throat if you are given to appetite") is about not being ensnared by the deceptive hospitality of rich hosts. And the saying in Philippians 3:19 ("their god is their belly") is either a euphemism for sexual sin (see the next phrase, "they glory in their shame") or a reference to the Judaizer's legalistic demands regarding Mosaic dietary restrictions.

So what does the sin of gluttony look like? When we take time to open our Bibles and read the relevant passages, we find that gluttony is much more than eating an entire bag of Double

Stuf Oreos. Partaking in food is much less of a concern than partaking in sexual sin (1 Cor. 6:13). The composite picture from the passages above suggests that a glutton is a loafer, a partyer, and a profligate. He's the prodigal son wasting his life on riotous living. She's the girl on spring break who thinks the pinnacle of human existence is to eat, drink, and hook up. A wastrel living for the weekend. A big-city highflier who cares for nothing except that he might indulge in high society. A ne'er-do-well who takes lifestyle cues from the *Hangover* franchise.

So, absolutely, the church should speak against the sin of gluttony. But once we understand what the sin entails, it seems likely most people have a good idea where the church already stands on these issues.

What God Has Joined Together

If the sin of gluttony has been misunderstood, what about divorce? This is a more serious charge laid at the feet of conservative evangelicals. In talking about homosexuality over the years I can't count all the times I've heard something like: "It's easy for you to pick on homosexuality because that's not the issue in your church. But you don't follow the letter of your own law. If you did, you would be talking about divorce, since that's the bigger problem in conservative churches." We have to admit the charge against us has been, for too long and in too many places, unfortunately and painfully accurate. We've grown accustomed to dispensable marriages. We've made peace with the disastrous shift that took place in the 1960s and '70s when our legislatures gave men and women the unilateral ability to end their marriages under the illusion of "no-fault" divorce.[4] Maybe we've tried to make a difference in the legal system, but to no avail.

---

[4] See Jennifer Roback Morse, "Why Unilateral Divorce Has No Place in a Free Society" in *The Meaning of Marriage: Family, State, Market, and Morals,* eds. Robert P. George and Jean Bethke Elshtain (Dallas, TX: Spence Publishing, 2006), 74–99.

Maybe we wanted to emphasize God's grace for those who re-gret their past mistakes. Maybe we saw so much divorce around us (or were in the midst of it), that we found it easier to look past Jesus's admonitions as nothing but wild hyperbole. It's true: divorce is a serious problem in Christ's church.

And yet, there are important differences between divorce and homosexuality. For starters, the biblical prohibition against divorce explicitly allows for exceptions (Matt. 5:32; 19:9; 1 Cor. 7:10–16); the prohibition against homosexuality does not. The traditional Protestant position, as stated in the *West-minster Confession of Faith* for example, maintains that divorce is permissible on grounds of marital infidelity or desertion by an unbelieving spouse.[5] Granted, the application of these prin-ciples is difficult and the question of remarriage after divorce gets even trickier, but most Christians have held that divorce is sometimes acceptable. Simply put, homosexuality and divorce are not identical because according to the Bible the former is always wrong, while the latter is not. Every divorce is the result of sin, but not every divorce is sinful.

Moreover, many Christians *do* take divorce seriously. A lot of the same churches that speak out against homosexuality also speak out against illegitimate divorce. I've preached on divorce a number of times and recently distributed to my con-gregation a paper entitled "What Did Jesus Think of Divorce and Remarriage?"[6] I've said more about homosexuality in the blogosphere because there's a controversy around the issue in the culture and in the wider church. But I've never shied away from talking about divorce.

As a board of elders, we steadfastly do *not* ignore this issue. We ask new members who have been divorced to explain the

---

[5] WCF 24.5–6.

[6] The paper is available on my blog at TGC, "A Sermon on Divorce and Remarriage," Novem-ber 3, 2010, http://www.thegospelcoalition.org/blogs/kevindeyoung/2010/11/03/a-sermon-on -divorce-and-remarriage/.

nature of their divorce and (if applicable) their remarriage. This has resulted on occasion in potential new members leaving our church. Many of the discipline cases we've encountered as elders have been about divorce. The majority of pastoral care crises we have been involved in have dealt with failed or failing marriages. Our church, like many others, takes seriously all kinds of sins, including illegitimate divorce. We don't always know how to handle every situation, but I can say with a completely clear conscience that we never turn a blind eye to divorce.

Again, undoubtedly many evangelicals have been negligent in dealing with illegitimate divorce and remarriage. Pastors have not preached on the issue for fear of offending scores of their members. Elder boards have not practiced church discipline on those who sin in this area because, well, they don't practice discipline for much of anything. Counselors, friends, and small groups have not gotten involved early enough to make a difference in predivorce situations. Christian attorneys have not thought enough about their responsibility in encouraging marital reconciliation. Church leaders have not helped their people understand God's teaching about the sanctity of marriage, and we have not helped those already wrongly remarried to experience forgiveness for their past mistakes.

So yes, there are plank-eyed Christians among us. The evangelical church, in many places, gave up and caved in on divorce and remarriage. But the remedy to this negligence is not more negligence. The slow, painful cure is more biblical exposition, more active pastoral care, more consistent discipline, more Word-saturated counseling, and more prayer—for illegitimate divorce, for same-sex behavior, and for all the other sins that are more easily condoned than confronted.

9

"The Church Is Supposed to Be a Place for Broken People"

A few years ago a major news story featured an important Christian leader who shut down his ministry to those with same-sex attraction. The story made national headlines because this man, who had previously identified himself as "ex-gay," was questioning whether those inclined toward same-sex sexual relationships could actually change and whether the conversation therapy used in his ministry did more harm than good.[1] Along with this change in ministry strategy came a new emphasis in theology. Although this leader continued to insist that homosexual behavior was wrong, he felt confident that those in homosexual relationships could still know the grace of God—whether they turned from their homosexual practice or not. He maintained that as long as we believe in Christ, the

---

[1] In my estimation, rethinking their method was called for, even if this individual went too far in the other direction in assuming the near immutability of a homosexual orientation. I put the term "ex-gay" in quotation marks because I'm not sure the man in question would still use that term or that it's even helpful. Some object to the term because they don't think lasting change is possible. Others refuse to use the term because they would rather find their identity in Christ, not in a sexual orientation (even a transformed one).

sexual choices we make do not interrupt our relationship with Christ. Whether we make the choice to walk in God's ways or pursue something less than God's best for us, we are still saved by Christ and will spend eternity with Christ. No one's perfect. We all fall short of the glory of God. We're all desperately in need of God's grace. But God's grace is unconditional, and the church is supposed to be a place for broken people, right?

Repent, for the Kingdom of Heaven Is at Hand

Yes and amen. We all need to be forgiven. We all need grace. The church is supposed to be full of sinners. But—and here's the rub—the communicant membership of the church, like the membership of heaven, is made up of born again, *repentant* sinners. If we preach a "gospel" with no call to repentance, we are preaching something other than the apostolic gospel. If we knowingly allow unconcerned, impenitent sinners into the membership and ministry of the church, we are deceiving their souls and putting ours at risk as well. If we think people can find a Savior without forsaking their sin, we do not know what sort of Savior Jesus Christ is. "Such were some of you" is the hope-filled call to holiness for the sexual sinner and for every other kind of sinner (1 Cor. 6:11).

Few things are more important in life than repentance. It is so important that the Gospels and the Epistles and the Old Testament make clear that you don't go to heaven without it. Ezekiel said, "Repent and turn from your transgressions" (Ezek. 18:30). John the Baptist said, "Repent, for the kingdom of heaven is at hand" (Matt. 3:2). Jesus said, "Repent and believe in the gospel" (Mark 1:15). Peter said, "Repent and be baptized" (Acts 2:38). And Paul said God "commands all people everywhere to repent" (Acts 17:30). No doubt, the church is for broken and imperfect people—broken people who hate what is broken in them and imperfect people who have renounced their sinful imperfections. If those with same-sex attraction are being singled out for repentance, the solution is not to remove forsaking of sin from the gospel equation, but to labor for a church community where lifelong repentance is the normal experience of Christian discipleship.

No one likes to be told, "Even now the axe is laid to the root of the trees. Every tree therefore that does not bear good fruit is cut down and thrown into the fire" (Luke 3:9). That's never been an easy sell. It's much easier to get a crowd by leaving out the repentance part of conversion, but it's not faithful to Christ. It's not even Christianity. We must show fruit in keeping with repentance (v. 8). Of course, there is a lot more to following Jesus than repentance, but it's certainly not less. "Repent," Jesus said, or "you will all likewise perish" (Luke 13:5).

Regret is common enough; repentance is rare. True Spirit-wrought repentance entails a break with the old and the start of something new. That's what the Greek word *metanoia* means— a change of mind that results in a change of life.

- You change your mind about *yourself*: "I am not fundamentally a good person deep down. I am not the center of the universe. I am not the king of the world or even my life."
- You change your mind about *sin*: "I am responsible for my actions. My past hurts do not excuse my present failings. My offenses against God and against others are not trivial. I do not live or think or feel as I should."
- You change your mind about *God*: "He is trustworthy. His word is sure. He is able to forgive and to save. I believe in his Son, Jesus Christ. I owe him my life and my allegiance. He is my King and my Sovereign, and he wants what is best for me. I will follow him no matter the cost."

- And then *you* change as God works in you to work out your salvation with fear and trembling (Phil. 2:12–13).

Free Grace Is Not Cheap

If we are to be faithful to Scripture, we must not provide assurance of salvation to those who are habitually, freely, and impenitently engaged in sinful activity. The Bible's teaching on this matter is as clear as it is unpopular: persistent unrepentant sexual sin leads people to hell (Matt. 5:27–32; Rom. 1:18–2:11; 1 Cor. 6:9–10; Gal. 5:19–21; 1 Thess. 4:3–8; cf. 1 John 3:4–10). When the man in Corinth was found sleeping with his father's wife, Paul's response was not "we all make mistakes" or "thank God for his unconditional love." Paul told the Corinthians to mourn over the sin (1 Cor. 5:2), to deliver this man to Satan for the destruction of his flesh (v. 5), to no longer associate with the immoral man (vv. 9–11), and to purge the evil person from among them (v. 13). Of course, Paul's aim was that through church discipline the man's spirit would be saved in the day of the Lord (v. 5), but this gracious hoped-for ending is not possible apart from repentance (6:9–11).

Dietrich Bonhoeffer, the German theologian and martyr, exposed the emptiness of repentance-less faith in his famous denunciation of cheap grace.

> [Cheap grace is] the grace which amounts to the justification of sin without the justification of the repentant sinner who departs from sin and from whom sin departs. Cheap grace is not the kind of forgiveness of sin which frees us from the toils of sin. Cheap grace is the grace we bestow on ourselves. Cheap grace is the preaching of forgiveness without requiring repentance, baptism without church discipline, Communion without confession, absolution without personal confession. Cheap grace is grace without

discipleship, grace without the cross, grace without Jesus Christ, living and incarnate.[2]

It's strange that some Christians would treat homosexual activity as an imperfect but allowable choice or simply less than God's best when we would never speak so dismissively about the sin of ethnic prejudice, economic exploitation, or violence against women. True religion is to visit orphans and widows in their affliction *and* to keep oneself unstained from the world (James 1:27). Which is another way of saying "faith apart from works is dead" (2:26). We cannot live like the Devil on earth and expect to meet God in heaven. This is not because God demands a certain number of holiness points in order to be saved. We are justified by faith alone through grace alone in Christ alone. *And* this grace that grants us faith will invariably be a grace that causes us to change. To ignore the second half of the previous sentence is to prove the first half never happened.

So does this mean God's love is conditional? That depends: are we talking about common grace (which all people enjoy) or saving grace (which only the redeemed experience)? A better question might be: is our final glorification conditional? If *conditional* means we have to earn our way to heaven, or that those declared righteous before God are in danger of being declared unrighteous on the day of judgment, then the answer is no. But *conditional* in the sense that we will not be glorified irrespective of the kind of life we live—then yes. The New Testament warnings are not indicative of a salvation that can be lost, but of a faith that must persevere. No matter how many times we walk an aisle or pray a prayer—no matter how many times we feel like we've been saved or how long it's been since we thought we were saved—the promise of appearing before God as holy and blameless is dependent upon continuing in the faith

---

[2] Dietrich Bonhoeffer, *The Cost of Discipleship* (New York: Macmillan, 1969 [1949]), 47.

that is stable and steadfast (Col. 1:22–23). We must make our calling and election sure (2 Pet. 1:10). As God keeps us from stumbling, so we must keep ourselves in the love of God and the mercy of our Lord Jesus Christ that leads to eternal life (Jude 21, 24). All of which is to disagree with those who think unrepentant sexual sin is consistent with Christian discipleship and to agree with the author of Hebrews, who taught that without holiness no one will see the Lord (12:14). Or to put it another way, we can simply agree with Jesus when he said, "The one who endures to the end will be saved" (Matt. 24:13).

10

"You're on the Wrong Side of History"

When Christians maintain that homosexual behavior is sinful or that marriage can only be between a man and a woman, you can count on a chorus of voices declaring confidently that these old views are on the "wrong side of history." The phrase is meant to sting. It conjures up pictures of segregationists clinging to their disgusting notions of racial supremacy. We are meant to think of the church persecuting Galileo or of flat-earthers warning Columbus about sailing off the edge of the world. The phrase seeks to win an argument by not having one. It says, "Your ideas are so laughably backward, they don't deserve to be taken seriously. In time everyone who ever held them will be embarrassed."

No doubt, the "wrong side of history" retort can feel like a heavy burden to bear. But is it true? Can we who live in the present be certain how our ideas will be viewed in the future? What if the unfolding of history is not nearly as neat as we think and the choosing of winners and losers not as tidy as we imagine?

Think about the hidden arguments in the phrase "wrong side of history."

The phrase assumes a progressive view of history that is empirically false and as a methodology has been thoroughly discredited. Academic historians often warn against what British historian and philosopher Herbert Butterfield labeled "Whig history," a term that gets its name from British political debates of the seventeenth century.[1] In Whig history the past is seen as an inexorable march from darkness to light, from bondage to liberty, and from ignorance into enlightenment. Like some Marxist views, Whig history presupposes the rationality of man and the inevitability of progress. It assumes that history is always moving in the same direction. But of course, history is never that simple, and knowing the future is never that easy, which is why Whig history is almost universally frowned upon by serious historians. The Whiggish approach, with its presumption of enlightenment and perpetual progress, is not the best way to understand the past and not by itself an adequate way to make sense of the present.

The phrase "wrong side of history" also forgets that progressive ideas can prove just as disastrous as traditional ones. To cite but one example, it was progressives in the early twentieth century who, in trying to applying Darwin's biological theories, championed racial determinism and eugenics (i.e., measures designed to promote the breeding of desirable characteristics). Many of the elite intellectuals of the day accepted "scientific" theories about innate mental differences among the races, as leaders on the left argued for eliminating the "inferior stock" of mankind through restricted immigration, institutionalization, and mass sterilization.[2] If there is a "wrong side of

---

[1] Herbert Butterfield, *The Whig Interpretation of History* (London: George Bell, 1931).
[2] See Thomas Sowell, *Intellectuals and Race* (New York: Basic Books, 2013), 21–43.

history," there are enough examples in history to tell us that anyone from any intellectual tradition could be on it.

Moreover, the "wrong side of history" argument usually perpetuates half-truths and misinformation about Christian history. For example, the church did not object to Columbus's voyage because it thought the earth was flat.[3] That's a myth that has been erroneously believed since John William Draper's *History of the Conflict between Religion and Science* (1874) and Andrew Dickson White's influential two-volume study, *A History of the Warfare of Science with Theology in Christendom* (1896). The "sundry wise men of Spain" who challenged Columbus did not do so because of their belief in the earth's flatness, but because they thought Columbus had underestimated the circumference of the earth, which he had.[4] Every educated person in Columbus's day knew the earth was round. Jeffrey Burton Russell argues that during the first fifteen centuries of the Christian era "nearly unanimous scholarly opinion pronounced the earth spherical, and by the fifteenth century all doubt had disappeared."[5] The Venerable Bede (673–735) taught that the world was round, as did Bishop Virgilius of Salzburg (ca. 700–784), Hildegard of Bingen (1098–1179), and Thomas Aquinas (1225–1274), all four of whom are canonized saints in the Catholic Church.

The received story about Galileo (1564–1642) is similarly misguided. Christians who defend homosexual activity often point to the work of the Italian physicist and astronomer as justification for rethinking the traditional understanding of marriage. "Look," it is said, "for 1600 years every Christian

---

[3] The paragraphs on Columbus and slavery are adapted from Kevin DeYoung and Ted Kluck, *Why We Love the Church: In Praise of Institutions and Organized Religion* (Chicago: Moody, 2009), 128–31.

[4] Rodney Stark, *For the Glory of God: How Monotheism Led to Reformations, Science, Witch-Hunts, and the End of Slavery* (Princeton: Princeton University Press, 2003), 121.

[5] Ibid., 122.

thought the Bible taught a geocentric universe. That's why the church persecuted Galileo. But once Christians embraced the insights of science and understood that the earth really revolved around the sun, they found a new and better way to interpret those Scriptural passages about sunrises and sunsets." This line of reasoning makes a valid point: we should always be willing to consider whether we've been misreading the Bible. The problem is that the history surrounding Galileo doesn't prove nearly as much as revisionists want it to prove.

For starters, the view that the sun revolved around the earth was not the product of theological and moral reflection. Ptolemy constructed his theory of a geocentric solar system in the second century AD based on Aristotle's ideas about the perfection of the heavens and the mutability of earth. Copernicus (more than Galileo) is usually the one said to have overturned Ptolemy, but the heliocentric view of the solar system (which is not the same as saying the earth moves) had already been developed in medieval scholastic universities. When Copernicus, who was a canon in the Church, published *On the Revolution of the Heavenly Spheres* (1543), he dedicated the book to the pope. Copernicus's work circulated freely for seventy years, with criticism coming chiefly from Aristotelian academics who thought the theories of Copernicus were beyond the pale of real science.

Galileo, for his part, was initially lauded by cardinals and welcomed by popes, establishing a good relationship with Pope Urban VIII, who wrote an ode in honor of the esteemed scientist. The relationship went sour when, in *Two Chief World Systems* (1632), Galileo put one of Urban's arguments in the mouth of the story's simpleton. This touched off a firestorm and sent Galileo to the pope's doghouse. In the end, Galileo was convinced that the main source of his trouble was making "fun of his Holiness" and not the matter of the earth moving.[6] Did the "Copernican revolution" help Christians make better sense of a few Bible passages? Perhaps, but to suggest that Galileo forced a reactionary church to finally get right what it had stubbornly gotten wrong for its entire history is hardly an unbiased reading of the historical circumstances.

And what about slavery? While it's true that Christians in the South often defended chattel slavery, this was not the position of the entire American church, and certainly not the universal position of the church throughout history. Unlike slavery, the church has always been convinced (until very recently) that homosexual behavior is sinful. There are no biblical passages that suggest the contrary. There are, however, passages in Scripture that encourage the freeing of slaves (Philem. 15–16) and condemn capturing another human being and selling him into slavery (Ex. 21:16; 1 Tim. 1:8–10). To make it sound like the Word of God is plainly for slavery in the same way it is plainly against homosexual practice is biblically indefensible.

Furthermore, it's not as if Christians never spoke against the institution until the nineteenth century.

- As early as the seventh century, Saith Bathilde (wife of King Clovis III) campaigned to stop slave-trading and free all slaves.
- In the ninth century Saint Anskar worked to halt the Viking slave trade.
- In the thirteenth century, Thomas Aquinas argued that slavery was a sin, a position upheld by a series of popes after him.
- In the fifteenth century, after the Spanish colonized the Canary Islands and began to enslave the native population, Pope Eugene IV issued a bull, giving everyone fifteen

---

[6] See Philip J. Sampson, *6 Modern Myths about Christianity and Western Civilization* (Downers Grove, IL: InterVarsity Press, 2001), 27–46.

days from receipt of his bull, "to restore to their earlier liberty all and each person of either sex who were once residents of said Canary Islands . . . these people are to be totally and perpetually free and are to be let go without exaction or reception of any money." The bull didn't help much, but that is owing to the weakness of the church's power at the time, not indifference to slavery. Pope Paul III made a similar pronouncement in 1537.

- Slavery was condemned in papal bulls in 1462, 1537, 1639, 1741, 1815, and 1839.
- In America, the first abolitionist tract was published in 1700 by Samuel Sewall, a devout Puritan.[7]

Clearly, the church's opposition to slavery is not a recent phenomenon. We do not find anything like this long track record when it comes to the church supporting homosexual practice.

I am not trying to rewrite history and make the record of the church into one long string of unbroken heroism. Clearly it isn't. Christians as individuals have been wrong about a great many things. And collectively in our local churches we've probably been wrong just as often. But to suggest—as those arguing for the acceptance of homosexual behavior must do—that the whole church has always, at all times, and in all places been wrong is an audacious claim, one that Protestants, Catholics, and Orthodox have never countenanced. As Christians we ought to fear being on the wrong side of the holy, apostolic, and universal church more than we fear being on the wrong side of discredited assumptions about progress and enlightenment.

---

[7] These bullet points rely on Stark, *For the Glory of God*, 329–39. The quotation from Pope Eugene IV is found on page 330.

11

"It's Not Fair"

I imagine many people struggle with the arguments in this book not because of a Greek word here or a particular verse there, but for a more visceral reason: it just doesn't feel fair. You may be thinking of a beloved brother or mother or aunt who has been in a homosexual relationship for years and seems quite happy and healthy. You may be thinking of your good friend from college who has been attracted to people of the same sex for as long as he can remember. You may be thinking of a son or daughter who just came out of the closet after many tears and many years of struggle. You may be thinking of yourself and your own failed attempts to get your desires to change. Whatever the situation, you can't help but think, "Why would God do this? Why would he give someone these desires and not allow them to be expressed? How can it be God's will for my mom, my son, my cousin, my friend to be unmarried and unfulfilled for the rest of their lives?"

These questions are not wrong. For many people they are personally poignant and extremely painful questions. I don't want to brush them off as unimportant. If someone from my congregation came to me with these questions, I would start by asking more questions and then hunker down for a lot of listening. I'd try to convey, however imperfectly, a sense of compassion and sympathy.

Our church, in the ten-plus years I've been here, has always had men and women who struggle with same-sex attraction. I've known most of them personally. Some of them have been friends. To be honest, some of the strugglers who once were a part of our church may no longer believe what they did when they were here. There are former church members, and some family members, who will strongly dislike this book. Many others—including those who continue to live celibate lives in the midst of same-sex desires—will be thankful for it. I don't expect anyone to listen to me just because I've had friends, family members, and people in the church identify as gay or lesbian. But I hope the skeptical will at least recognize that this issue is not one I've kept comfortably at arm's length. Pastors in today's world cannot ignore these questions of fairness and still be faithful and effective in caring for their flocks.

Let me tackle the fairness objection by looking at it in three common forms.

It's Not Fair—I Was Born This Way

According to the American Psychiatric Association, "the causes of sexual orientation (whether homosexual or heterosexual) are not known at this time and likely are multifactorial including biological and behavioral roots which may vary between different individuals and may even vary over time." Likewise the American Psychological Association has concluded: "Although much research has examined the possible genetic, hormonal, developmental, social, and cultural influences on sexual orientation, no findings have emerged that permit scientists to conclude that sexual orientation is determined by any particular factor or factors."[1] This is not to suggest that those with same-sex attraction woke up one day and decided to feel the way they feel. In most cases it seems that same-sex desires are not consciously chosen. Why these desires emerge in a small subset of the population is not entirely known or agreed upon. The claim that homosexuality can be tied to a fixed hereditary or biological trait cannot be supported by the scientific evidence.

Even if biological causes for homosexuality could be isolated—and even if the desires almost always come unbidden—these factors do not remove culpability from the equation. We are all products of nature and nurture. We all struggle with desires that should not be fulfilled and with longings for things illicit. As Christians we know that the heart is desperately wicked (Jer. 17:9). We are fallen people with a propensity for sin and self-deception. We cannot derive oughts from what is.

Our own sense of desire and delight, or of pleasure and of pain, is not self-validating. People may, through no conscious decision of their own, be drawn to binge drinking, to promiscuity, to rage, to self-pity, or to any number of sinful behaviors. If the "is-ness" of personal experience and desire determines the "ought-ness" of embracing these desires and acting upon them, there is no logical reason why other sexual "orientations" (say, toward children, or animals, or promiscuity, or bisexuality, or multiple partners) should be stigmatized.[2] As creatures made in the image of God, we are

---

[1] "Position Statement on Homosexuality," *American Psychiatric Association*, 2013, www
.psychiatry.org/File%20Library/Learn/Archives/ps2013_Homosexuality.pdf; http://www.apa.org
/topics/lgbt/orientation.pdf; "Answers to Your Questions: For a Better Understanding of Sexual
Orientation and Homosexuality," *American Psychological Association*, 2008, http://www.apa
.org/topics/lgbt/orientation.pdf. Thanks to Denny Burk for pointing me to these statements.

[2] "There is a growing conviction, notably in Canada, that paedophilia should probably be
classified as a distinct sexual orientation, like heterosexuality or homosexuality. Two eminent
researchers testified to that effect to a Canadian parliamentary commission last year, and the
Harvard Mental Health Letter of 2010 stated baldly that paedophilia 'is a sexual orientation'

moral beings, responsible for our actions and for the lusts of the flesh. Quite simply, sometimes we want the wrong things. No matter how we think we might have been born one way, Christ insists that we must be born again a different way (John 3:3–7; Eph. 2:1–10).

Sexual orientation is not an immutable part of our biology like a hitchhiker's thumb or the presence of a Y chromosome. If it were, the concordance rate would not be so low between identical twins (i.e., both twins would always have the same sexual orientation, which is not the case).[3] No doubt, many persons with same-sex desires, despite efforts to the contrary, will experience these desires throughout their lives. But others have experienced everything from partial to radical sexual transformation. I think of Rosaria Butterfield, the postmodern lesbian professor who became a Reformed Christian and homeschooling mother.[4] Or of my friend Ron Citlau, a husband, father, and pastor whose early life was marked by intense drug use and promiscuous same-sex behavior.[5] Or of the Christian rapper-poet Jackie Hill-Perry, who had same-sex attractions as early as five years old and is now a wife and mother.[6] I'm not suggesting that these kinds of drastic sexual transformations are easy or even normal, but they do (and can) happen.

---

and therefore 'unlikely to change'" (Jon Henley, "Paedophilia: Bringing Dark Desires to Light," *The Guardian*, January 3, 2013, http://www.theguardian.com/society/2013/jan/03/paedophilia -bringing-dark-desires-light).

[3] Khytam Dawood, J. Michael Bailey, and Nicholas G. Martin, "Genetic and Environmental Influences on Sexual Orientation," in *Handbook of Behavior Genetics*, Yong-Kyu Kim, ed., (New York: Springer, 2009), 271–72.

[4] Rosaria Butterfield, *The Secret Thoughts of an Unlikely Convert: An English Professor's Journey into the Christian Faith*, 2nd edition (Pittsburgh, PA: Crown and Covenant, 2014).

[5] Adam T. Barr and Ron Citlau, *Compassion without Compromise: How the Gospel Frees Us to Love Our Gay Friends without Losing the Truth* (Minneapolis, MN: Bethany, 2014), 1416. See also the resources available through www.loveintolight.com and the book of the same title, *Love into Light*, by Peter Hubbard (Greenville, SC: Ambassador International, 2013).

[6] Jackie Hill, "Love Letter to a Lesbian," Desiring God, May 16, 2013, www.desiringgod.org /blog/posts/love-letter-to-a-lesbian.

It's Not Fair—I Don't Have the Gift of Celibacy

So what about all the instances in which those with same-sex attraction never seem to feel that "spark" for persons of the opposite sex? Then what? Some people may choose to marry someone of the opposite sex even without a strong sense of sexual attraction. Others will resonate with Sam Allberry, a single Anglican pastor with same-sex attraction, who has concluded that for him the only Christian alternative is to embrace a life of hope-filled celibacy. Sam is right: heterosexual marriage is the only proper context for sexual intimacy, no matter how strongly or how persistently or how achingly we may wrestle with unfulfilled sexual desires.[7]

But isn't celibacy a gift from God that he grants only to some Christians? That's one of the most popular arguments from the revisionist side. Paul said he had a unique gift, but others didn't, and those who didn't were supposed to marry rather than burn with passion (1 Cor. 7:7–9). So how we can ask those without the gift of celibacy to live a life God has not called them to? At least single heterosexuals have the hope of getting married. Traditionalists are telling those in the gay community that their dreams of experiencing love and marriage will never be fulfilled. We are functionally castrating them. Celibacy, according to the revisionist, must be a choice. And yet, the church has insisted those who experience same sex attraction should not be sexually intimate with those of the same sex. It's a burden greater than they can bear (1 Cor. 10:13).

While we should not minimize the struggle those with homosexual desires have to remain chaste, the revisionist logic fails on several accounts.

(1) It assumes that homosexual desires cannot change, so

---

[7] Sam Allberry, *Is God Anti-Gay? And Other Questions about Homosexuality, the Bible, and Same-Sex Attraction* (Purcellville, VA: The Good Book Company, 2013), 48–49.

that, consequently, marriage is an utter impossibility. We've already seen that this is not always the case. Jean Lloyd, who began to experience same-sex attraction at the age of twelve and is now in her forties, went from "being closeted to openly lesbian to celibate to heterosexually married." She writes, "Over many years, my experience of same-sex attraction went from being a continual fire to an occasional flicker. A man who still experiences same-sex attraction but is happily married to a woman, where he saw no possibility of a heterosexual relationship before, has indeed changed."[8]

(2) The revisionist case also overstates the sexual freedom found in marriage. To be sure, intimacy in marriage is a precious gift, and it does provide an outlet for sexual desire. But even in the happiest of homes, marriage itself is not a sufficient outlet for all sexual desire. Every married man I know still wrestles with some measure of not-to-be-fulfilled sexual desire. The temptation to sexual sin does not end when you say "I do." Resisting sexual desire is a part of discipleship for every Christian, no matter our marital status and no matter the kinds of attractions we experience. Desire must never be given the priority over obedience. Intense longing does not turn sinful wrongs into civil rights.

(3) The revisionist logic proves too much. If chastity is too much to ask of the person with same-sex sexual desires, then it is too much to ask of the person with heterosexual desires. What about the single Christian woman who never finds a husband? Or the godly man whose wife is paralyzed at thirty years old, making sexual intimacy an impossibility? Did these believers choose the gift of celibacy? How many of their dreams will go unfulfilled?

(4) Finally, the revisionist argument rests on a misunder-

---

[8] Jean Lloyd, "Seven Things I Wish My Pastor Knew about My Homosexuality," *Public Discourse*, December 10, 2014, http://www.thepublicdiscourse.com/2014/12/14149/.

standing of 1 Corinthians 7. The parallel in verse 7—"each has his own gift, one of one kind and one of another"—is not, strictly speaking, a reference to celibacy and marriage themselves. Rather the contrast in verse 7 is between "the gift of a positive attitude which makes the most of the freedoms of celibacy without frustration, and the positive attitude which caringly provides the responsibilities, intimacies, love, and 'dues' of marriage while equally living out the gospel."[9] The decision to obey God and enjoy sexual intimacy only in the context of marriage between a man and a woman is not dependent upon a special gift from God. When the single person, however, embraces the advantages of being single and the gospel opportunities unique to singleness, this is considered a *charisma* given by the Spirit for the edification of the body (7:32–35; 12:7). It's unthinkable that the Paul who just argued that those who practice homosexuality will not inherit the kingdom (6:9–10) and that a *man* should have his own *wife* and each *woman* her own *husband* (7:2) would now be suggesting that people with strong homosexual desires should be able to satisfy those desires if sexual purity seems too onerous.

It's Not Fair—God Wouldn't Want Me to Be So Miserable

What about the experience of those who have found themselves feeling happier and healthier once they stopped fight-

---

[9] Anthony C. Thiselton, *The First Epistle to the Corinthians*, New International Greek Testament Commentary (Grand Rapids, MI: Eerdmans, 2000), 513–14. Likewise, Roy E. Ciampa and Brian S. Rosner: "In v. 7 the *gift* from God is not celibacy itself, especially conceived of as a perpetual state. . . . [T]he states of celibacy/singleness and marriage are common gifts of providence to all creation. When Paul talks of 'gifts' in his letters, he means those having reference not to creation but to the new creation of the kingdom and the gospel, gifts that carry responsibilities specifically to God and to God's people. The gifts that Paul has in mind in v. 7 refer to the contentedness contributing to a life of service rather than to a lifelong calling to 'eunuch-hood' (cf. Matt. 19:12)" (*The First Letter to the Corinthians* [Grand Rapids, MI: Eerdmans, 2010], 285–86).

ing their same-sex desires? The revisionist literature is replete with stories of those in the gay community who used to be miserable and full of despair, sometimes (as they describe it) because they were surrounded by nonaffirming churches and families. When they tried to change their sexuality or embrace lifelong celibacy, they never felt close to God and never experienced the peace that passes understanding. In many cases, those with homosexual feelings describe growing up with a hatred for their own bodies and an initial disgust for their own desires. Their lives were often marked by depression, confusion, and sometimes even suicidal thoughts. But, as the stories go, once they learned to embrace their God-given identity and reconcile their faith with their sexual orientation, many "gay Christians" have discovered a new vibrancy in their walk with God. If embracing their sexuality were really a step away from God, revisionist authors ask, why are so many "gay Christians" spiritually flourishing? A healthy tree cannot bear bad fruit, and a diseased tree does not bear good fruit (Matt. 7:18). How are we supposed to explain the presence of kind, generous, sacrificial men and women who follow Christ *and* live in committed same-sex relationships? It doesn't make sense to condemn homosexuality when so many Christians are made miserable by repressing their sexual orientation, only to become more joyful and more effective in ministry when they learn to accept it.

Again, it bears repeating: personal experience is not unimportant. No matter our position on this issue (or any issue), churches and pastors should not be indifferent to the cries of those who profess Christ and profess to be miserable at the same time. We can't help but pay attention to our pain, but we should not think that God always says what we want him to say in the midst of our pain. The Bible has to have the last word on what is good for us and what brings glory to God. As Jackie Hill-Perry puts it in her "Love Letter to a Lesbian":

> You see what God has to say about homosexuality, but your heart doesn't utter the same sentiments. God's word says it's sinful; your heart says it feels right. God's word says it's abominable; your heart says it's delightful. God's word says it's unnatural; your heart says it's totally normal. Do you see that there is a clear divide between what God's word says and how your heart feels?[10]

Given the corrupting effects of the fall and the human propensity for self-deception, we must base our ethical decision on something more than our subjective sense of what feels right. What about the woman who leaves an unhappy marriage, marries the man she was having an affair with, and after the unbiblical divorce and remarriage claims that she's never felt closer to God? What about the man who feels unfulfilled when he hasn't looked at porn in two weeks? Or what about all the sweet Christians who do lots of good things in the church while still holding racist views about African Americans? Are any of these sins made acceptable because the person committing them feels they are quite natural?

The "good fruit" Jesus talks about in Matthew 7:15–20 is not a reference to my sense of satisfaction or my perceived ministry effectiveness. The next verses make clear that laboring in Jesus's name, even with impressive results, is no guarantee of entering the kingdom of heaven (vv. 21–23). Bearing fruit means doing the will of our Father who is in heaven (v. 21). Jesus is looking for followers who will hear his words and put them into practice (vv. 24–27). No matter what we feel about ourselves or what others think about our effectiveness in the

---

[10] Hill-Perry, "Love Letter to a Lesbian."

church, there are no genuinely healthy trees apart from obedience to Christ and the fruit of the Spirit (Gal. 5:16–24).

Putting Sex in Perspective

I don't deny these are hard sayings for people with same-sex desires and for their friends and family. Jesus had a fondness for saying hard things. He told his disciples it was not enough to simply confess the right things about the Messiah. If they were to be true disciples, they had to deny themselves, take up their cross, and follow him (Matt. 16:17, 23, 24). Try to save your life, and you'll lose it. Be willing to lose your life, and you'll find it (v. 25). The grace which leads us to say yes to our great God and Savior Jesus Christ also demands that we say no to ungodliness and worldly passions (Titus 2:11–14).

Dying to self is the duty of every follower of Christ. I have my own struggles, my own sins, and my own suffering. We all do. We have all been distorted by original sin. We all show signs of "not the way things are supposed to be." We all groan for the redemption of our bodies (Rom. 8:23). We all long for creation to be set free from its bondage to corruption and obtain the freedom of the glory of the children of God (v. 21). This does not minimize the struggle of those who experience same-sex attraction, but it is does maximize the ways in which we are more alike than different. Grief and groaning, longing and lament, sorrowful yet always rejoicing—it's the life we live between two worlds. The church has long known about the pain of persecution, infertility, betrayal, injustice, addiction, famine, depression, and death. The church is just beginning to learn about the pain of living with unwanted same-sex attraction. For a growing number of Christians it is part of their cross to bear.

And it should not be carried alone. Singleness—and that will be the path of obedience for many who experience same-sex attraction—does not mean you must live alone, die alone, never hold a hand, never have a hug, and never know the touch of another human being. If we ask the single Christian to be chaste, we can only ask them to carry that cross in community. Perhaps *single* is not even the best term for those whom we expect live a full life in the midst of friends and colaborers. If God sets the lonely in families, so should we (Ps. 68:6 NIV). There is no reason the dire scenes painted by the revisionist side must be realized. With openness about the struggle and openness toward the struggler, those Christians in our midst who experience same-sex attraction need not be friendless, helpless, and hopeless.

But, of course, none of this can be possible without uprooting the idolatry of the nuclear family, which holds sway in many conservative churches. The trajectory of the New Testament is to *relativize* the importance of marriage and biological kinship. A spouse and a minivan full of kids on the way to Disney World is a sweet gift and a terrible god. If everything in Christian community revolves around being married with children, we should not be surprised when singleness sounds like a death sentence.

If that's the church's challenge, what's needed in the wider culture is a deep demythologizing of sex. Nothing in the Bible encourages us to give sex the exalted status it has in our culture, as if finding our purpose, our identity, and our fulfillment all rest on what we can or cannot do with our private parts. Jesus is the fullest example of what it means to be human, and he never had sex. How did we come to think that the most intense emotional attachments and the most fulfilling aspects of life can only be expressed with sexual intimacy?

In the Christian vision of heaven, there is no marriage in the blessed life to come (Luke 20:34–35). Marital intimacy is but a shadow of a brighter, more glorious reality, the marriage of Jesus Christ to his bride, the church (Rev. 19:6–8). If sexual intimacy is nothing up there, how can we make it to be every-thing down here? It would be terribly unfair for the church to tell those with same-sex desires that they are not fully human and cannot pursue a fully human life. But if the *summum bonum* of human existence is defined by something other than sex, the hard things the Bible has to say to those with same-sex desires is not materially different from the hard things it has to say to everyone else.

12

"The God I Worship Is a God of Love"

The God of the Bible is profoundly and propositionally a God of love. He is merciful and gracious, slow to anger and abounding in steadfast love (Ps. 103:8). He so loved the world that he gave his only Son, that whoever believes in him should not perish but have eternal life (John 3:16). The love of God was made manifest among us, that God sent his only Son into the world, so that we might live through him (1 John 4:9). God is love (v. 16).

Without denying or minimizing one iota of these precious biblical truths, it also needs to be made clear that the love of God does not swallow up all the other divine attributes. We'd do well to reconsider the doctrine of divine simplicity.[1] By "simple" we do not mean that God is slow or dim-witted. Nor do we mean that God is easy to understand. *Simple*, as a divine attribute, is the opposite of *compound*. The simplicity of God

---

[1] The oldest of the doctrinal standards of the Reformed churches, the *Belgic Confession* (1561), begins with the declaration "that there is a single and simple spiritual being, whom we call God" (article 1).

means that God is not *made up* of his attributes. He does not *consist* of goodness, mercy, justice, and power. He *is* goodness, mercy, justice, and power. Every attribute of God is identical with his essence.

This means we'd be wrong to insist that love is the true *nature* of God while omnipotence (or holiness or sovereignty or whatever) is only an *attribute* of God. This is a common error, and one which the doctrine of simplicity would help us avoid. We often hear people say, "God may *have* justice or wrath, but the very essence of God *is* love." The implication is that love is more central to the nature of God, more true to his real identity, than other less essential attributes. But this is to imagine God as a composite being instead of a simple being. It is perfectly appropriate to highlight the love of God when Scripture makes it such a central theme. But the declaration "God is love" (1 John 4:8) does not carry more metaphysical weight than "God is light" (1 John 1:5), "God is spirit" (John 4:24), "God is a consuming fire" (Heb. 12:29), or, for that matter, statements about God's goodness, kindness, power, or omniscience. Moral judgments against homosexuality cannot be outflanked by the argument, "Yeah, but God *is* love." The simplicity of God prevents us from ranking certain attributes higher or more essential than others.

Jesus the Intolerant

Just as crucially, we cannot settle for a culturally imported understanding of love. The steadfast love of God must not be confused with a blanket affirmation or an inspirational pep talk. No halfway responsible parent would ever think that loving her child means affirming his every desire and finding ways to fulfill whatever wishes he deems important. Parents generally know better what their kids really need, just like God *always* knows how we ought to live and who we ought to be. Christians cannot be tolerant of all things because God is not tolerant of all things. We can respect differing opinions and treat our opponents with civility, but we cannot give our unqualified, unconditional affirmation to every belief and behavior. We must love what God loves. That's where the church at Ephesus failed (Rev. 2:4). But we must also hate what God hates (v. 6). That's where Thyatira failed.

Of the seven cities in Revelation, Thyatira is the least well known. And yet, the letter is the longest of the seven. There was a lot going on at this church—some bad, some good.

Let's start with the good. In verse 19 Jesus says, "I know your works, your love and faith and service and patient endurance." Ephesus was praised for its good deeds and strong work ethic. In some ways, Thyatira was even better. It had the deeds that Ephesus had and the love that Ephesus lacked. The church at Thyatira was not without genuine virtue. It was a tight-knit bunch who loved, served, believed, and endured.

Maybe Thyatira was the kind of church you walked into and immediately felt like you belonged: "Great to meet you. Come, let me introduce you to my friends. I'll show you how you can get plugged in, use your gifts, do ministry. We're so glad you're here." It was a caring church, a sacrificial church, a loving church. That was the good part.

And the bad part? "But I have this against you, that you tolerate that woman Jezebel" (v. 20). Thyatira's love could be undiscerning and blindly affirming. The church tolerated false teaching and immoral behavior, two things God is fiercely intolerant of. Jesus says, "You're loving in many ways, but your tolerance is not love. It's unfaithfulness."

The specific sin in Thyatira was the tolerance of Jezebel. That wasn't the woman's real name. But this false prophetess was acting like the famous Old Testament Jezebel—leading people into adultery and idolatry. We don't know if this Thyatiran woman's influence was formal (she got up in front of people and told them deceptive things) or informal (she engaged in private conversations or her falsehoods spread by word of mouth). However it was happening, she was a spiritual danger, like her Old Testament namesake.

Jezebel (the actual Old Testament one) was the daughter of Ethbaal, King of the Sidonians. She worshiped Baal and Asherah and led her husband, Ahab, in the same. Jezebel is the one who plotted to kill innocent Naboth for his vineyard. She was called "that cursed woman" (2 Kings 9:34). As a punishment for her wickedness, she was eventually pushed out a window, trampled by horses, and eaten up by dogs. She was a bad lady. And she led many Israelites down a bad path.

Jesus says to Thyatira, "You are allowing a woman like that to have sway over your people. Why do you tolerate her? Don't affirm her. Don't dialogue with her. Don't wait and see what happens. Get rid of her . . . or I will." Apparently, by some means, the Lord had already warned her to repent, but she refused. And so now the Lord Jesus promises to throw her onto the sick bed and make her followers suffer, too, unless they repent. Jesus isn't messing around here. This isn't a secondary issue. Her wickedness was a serious sin worthy of death.

It was also an entrenched sin. Thyatira supported a number of trade guilds. Suppose you belonged to the local BAT, the Bricklayers Association of Thyatira, and one night the guild got together for a feast. You'd be sitting around the table, ready to partake of this great celebration with your friends and colleagues, and the host would say something like, "We're glad you could make it. What a happy occasion for the BAT. We have quite a feast prepared for you. But before we partake, we want to recognize the great god Zeus, who watches over the bricklayers and has made this dinner possible. Zeus—we see your statue in the corner—we eat to you, in your honor, for your worship. Let's dig in."

What would you do in that situation? Stay or go? What would your participation signify before your fellow Christians, before the watching world, before God? Christians in the ancient world didn't have to go searching for idolatry. It was woven into the fabric of their whole culture. To not participate in these pagan rituals was to invite ridicule and marginalization. These feasts, with their idolatry and the sexual revelry which would often follow, were a normal part of life in the Greco-Roman world. Removing yourself from them could be socially and economically disastrous.

This is why false teachers like the Jezebel in Thyatira, or the Nicolaitans in Pergamum, gained such a hearing. They made being a Christian much easier, much less costly, must less countercultural. But it was a compromised Christianity, and Jesus could not tolerate it. He was going to make an example of Thyatira to show all the churches that Jesus has eyes like fire (too pure to look on evil) and feet like burnished bronze (too holy to walk among wickedness). He wanted all the churches to know that he was the searcher of hearts and minds and he would repay evil for unrepentant evil, just as he would reward those who overcame the temptations of the surrounding culture and maintained their commitment to the truth (Rev. 2:26–28).

Show Me the Text

The debates about gender and sexuality are not going away. Whether you love the frenzied back and forth or (more likely) wish the whole big mess of controversy would magically disappear, that's just not the world we live in. The issues are too massive, the stakes too high, the feelings too intense for all of this to slip silently into the night. The world (and the church) will keep arguing about homosexual behavior and same-sex marriage and whether Jesus would go to a same-sex wedding. Fair enough. We live in a free country. In the public square (which is not the same as the boundaries of church membership or confessional commitment), we should expect a wild and woolly exchange of ideas and arguments.

But there's the rub. A rant is not an idea, and feeling hurt is not an argument. To be sure, how we make each other feel is not unimportant. But in our age of perpetual outrage, we must make clear that offendedness is not proof of the coherence or plausibility of any argument. Now is not the time for fuzzy thinking. Now is not the time to shy away from careful definitions. Now is not the time to let moods substitute for logic. These are difficult issues. These are personal issues. These are complicated issues. We cannot chart our ethical course by what feels better. We cannot build our theology based on what makes us look nicer. We cannot abdicate intellectual responsibility because smart people disagree.

And we certainly cannot keep our Bibles closed. We must submit ourselves to Scripture and let God be true even if it makes every man a liar (Rom. 3:4). After all, we can be inventors of evil (Rom. 1:30), but according to Jesus the Scriptures cannot be broken (John 10:35). We must be like the Bereans, who examined the Scriptures daily to see if what they were hearing should be believed (Acts 17:11). We must not settle for platitudes and slogans. It's easy to say things like "Love is more important than religion" or "God's grace is always surprising and scandalous" or "Jesus upset the traditionalists of his day and embraced the outcasts"—but what do any of these pious sounding phrases actually mean? Unless we explain what we mean by "love" and "religion" and "grace" and "traditionalists" and "embraced" and "outcasts," we're speaking in vacuous bromides. One could just as easily generalize from, say, the first chapter of the Sermon on the Mount that the world hates those committed to holiness (Matt. 5:10–12, 13), that the religious leaders of the first century were not religious enough (vv. 17–20), and that Jesus hated the ethical inclusivity of the Pharisees (vv. 21–48). Each of those statements could be true, but they demand definition and nuance. Sweeping statements of nebulous spiritual sentiment do not a worldview make. Show me the text—all the relevant texts. We must know the Bible better than to set aside specific verses because of general themes.

And so it is with the love of God. God is love, but this is quite different from affirming that our culture's understanding of love must be God.[2] "In this is love," John wrote, "not that we have loved God but that he has loved us and sent his Son to be the propitiation for our sins" (1 John 4:10). Love is what God did in sending his Son to be our substitute on the cross (Rom. 5:8). Love is what we do when we keep Christ's commands (John 14:15). Love is sharing with our brothers and sisters in need (1 John 3:16–18). Love is treating each other with kindness and patience (1 Cor. 13:4). Love is disciplining the wayward sinner (Prov. 3:11–12). Love is chastising the rebellious saint (Heb. 12:5–6). And love is throwing your arms around the prodigal son when he sees his sin, comes to his senses, and heads for home (Luke 15:17–24).

The God we worship is indeed a God of love. Which does not, according to any verse in the Bible, make sexual sin acceptable. But it does, by the witness of a thousand verses all over the Bible, make every one of our sexual sins changeable, redeemable, and wondrously forgivable.

---

[2] As Jean Lloyd, a former lesbian put it, "Continue to love me, but remember that you cannot be more merciful than God. It isn't mercy to affirm same-sex acts as good. . . . Don't compromise truth; help me to live in harmony with it" ("Seven Things I Wish My Pastor Knew about My Homosexuality," *Public Discourse*, December 10, 2014, http://www.thepublicdiscourse.com /2014/12/14149/).

Conclusion

Walking with God and Walking with Each Other in Truth and Grace

We don't get to pick the age we will live in, and we don't get to choose all the struggles we will face. Faithfulness is ours to choose; the shape of that faithfulness is God's to determine. In our time, faithfulness means (among a thousand other things) a patiently winsome and carefully reasoned restating of the formerly obvious: homosexual behavior is a sin. Along with most Christians around the globe and virtually every Christian in the first nineteen-and-a-half centuries of church history, I believe the Bible places homosexual behavior—no matter the level of commitment or mutual affection—in the category of sexual immorality. "To write the same things to you, in an age of purposeful forgetfulness, is no trouble to me and is safe for you," Paul might say (Phil. 3:1).

And yet, different people need to hear the same things in different ways and toward different ends. I'd like to think that everyone reading this book will weigh the arguments dispassionately and consider their merits based on carefully reasoned exegetical, historical, and theological conclusions. But I know it's difficult to read (or write) *any* book without personality and personal history coming through, let alone a book on such a highly charged controversial issue. That doesn't mean objectivity, clarity, and scriptural integrity are impossible. It does mean that in thinking through this issue each of us needs to consider our predilections and predispositions, where we've been, and where we need to go.

More Than You Might Think

For anyone about to bail on the millennia-old understanding of marriage, I hope you'll consider what's at stake. Because it's more than you might think.

The moral logic of monogamy is at stake. If three or thirteen or thirty people really love each other, why shouldn't they have a right to get married? And for that matter, why not a brother and a sister, or two sisters, or a mother and her son, or a father and his son, or any combination of two or more persons who love each other? I'm not suggesting this is what all, or even most, liberal Christians are arguing for. I am suggesting that there is no consistent logic to forestall this kind of argument. Jesus never spoke explicitly against polygamy. He never said anything against incest either. Maybe the New Testament authors only knew of exploitative polygamy. If they had known of committed, loving polygamous (multiple wives) or polyamorous (many lovers) relationships, who's to say they wouldn't have approved? Once we've accepted the logic that for love to be validated it must be expressed sexually and that those engaged in consensual sexual activity cannot be denied the "right" to marry, we have opened a Pandora's box of marital permutations that cannot be shut.

The integrity of Christian sexual ethics is at stake. The issue is bigger than just homosexuality. When one area of sexual ethics gets liberalized, the rest tends to get liberalized. Will those who have faulted traditionalists for being silent about heterosexual sins now speak out against premarital sex, marital infidelity, and unbiblical divorce, especially when these sins occur among those engaged in homosexual activity? Will those in the church who support homosexual practice, and those professing Christians engaged in homosexual practice, celebrate the Bible's high calling to personal holiness, or does the acceptance of homosexual behavior speak to a more pervasive declension of ethical standards?[1]

The authority of the Bible is at stake. It's not surprising that both sides, the traditionalist and the revisionist, have their "conversion" stories. On the one side, men and women leave behind a life of homosexual practice, and the other side, men and women leave behind a life of fundamentalism. Both kinds of stories have an I-once-was-blind-but-now-I-see feel to them: "I used to be a practicing homosexual, but then I submitted to God's Word and Jesus set me free." Or, "I used to think homosexuality was wrong, but then I realized how oppressive the expectations around me were and I went back to the Bible and discovered that the texts didn't mean what I thought they meant." I'm not saying that those on the revisionist side don't

---

[1] According to one study by a sociologist at the University of Texas, churchgoing Christians who *support* same-sex marriage were much more likely than churchgoing Christians who *oppose* same-sex marriage to agree or strongly agree that viewing pornography is OK (33.4 percent to 4.6 percent), that premarital cohabitation is good (37.2 percent to 10.9 percent), that no-strings-attached sex is OK (33.0 percent to 5.1 percent), and that it's OK for three or more adults to live in a sexual relationship (15.5 percent to 1.2 percent). Those in favor of same-sex marriage were also more likely to support abortion rights (39.1 percent to 6.5 percent). And each of these percentages was even higher when polling those who self-identify as gay and lesbian Christians—57 percent thought viewing pornography was permissible, 49.7 percent agreed that cohabitation before marriage was good, 49.0 percent believed no-strings-attached sex was OK, 31.9 percent were fine with polyamorous relationships, and 57.5 percent supported abortion rights (Mark Regnerus, "Tracking Christian Morality in a Same-Sex Marriage Future," *Public Discourse*, August 11, 2014, http://www.thepublicdiscourse.com/2014/08/13667/).

ever take the Bible seriously. Many of them do. But it's still the case that the turning point in coming to reject the historic view is often some sort of personal experience: a gay friend, a lesbian daughter, a homosexual church member, a sense of emptiness, a sense of happiness, a sense of closeness to God. In most of the instances I read where people changed their minds about homosexuality (either to embrace same-sex desires or to affirm those who do), it was first because of an experience, and then later because they concluded that the Bible didn't have to contradict what they had come to believe through their experience.

Luke Timothy Johnson, a well-respected New Testament scholar who supports homosexual behavior, speaks to the issue with refreshing candor:

> I think it important to state clearly that we do, in fact, reject the straightforward commands of Scripture, and appeal instead to another authority when we declare that same-sex unions can be holy and good. And what exactly is that authority? We appeal explicitly to the weight of our own experience and the experience thousands of others have witnessed to, which tells us that to claim our own sexual orientation is in fact to accept the way in which God has created us.[2]

There is a word for this: it's called liberalism. I don't mean that as a slam, but as a definitional matter of fact. Liberalism is both a tradition, coming out of the late eighteenth-century Protestant attempt to reconfigure traditional Christian teaching

---

[2] Luke Timothy Johnson, "Homosexuality and the Church: Scripture and Experience," *Commonweal.com*, June 11, 2007, https://www.commonwealmagazine.org/homosexuality -church-1. Similarly, Diarmaid MacCulloch, a decorated historian and gay man who left the church over the issue of homosexuality, has written: "This is an issue of biblical authority. Despite much well-intentioned theological fancy footwork to the contrary, it is difficult to see the Bible as expressing anything else but disapproval of homosexual activity, let alone having any conception of a homosexual identity. The only alternatives are either to try to cleave to patterns of life and assumptions set out in the Bible, or to say that in this, as in much else, the Bible is simply wrong" (*The Reformation: A History* [New York: Penguin, 2003], 705).

in the light of modern knowledge and values, and a diverse but recognizable approach to theology. Gary Dorrien, the foremost expert on American liberal theology and himself a part of that tradition, gives this definition:

> Fundamentally it is the idea of a genuine Christianity not based on external authority. Liberal theology seeks to reinterpret the symbols of Christianity in a way that creates a progressive religious alternative to atheistic rationalism and to theologies based on external authority. Specifically, liberal theology is defined by its openness to the verdicts of modern intellectual inquiry, especially the natural and social sciences; its commitment to the authority of individual reason and experience; its conception of Christianity as an ethical way of life; its favoring of moral concepts of atonement; and its commitment to make Christianity credible and socially relevant to modern people.[3]

Christians must know what liberalism is, not to be scared of it like the bogeyman, but so they can see what the lay of the land really looks like. The path which leads to the affirmation of homosexual behavior is a journey which inevitably leaves behind a clear, inerrant Bible, and picks up from liberalism a number of assumptions about the importance of individual authority and cultural credibility.

Finally, the grand narrative of Scripture is at stake. I'm not sure we're all telling the same story. A holy God sends his holy Son to die as an atoning sacrifice for unholy people so that by the power of the Holy Spirit they can live holy lives and enjoy God forever in the holy place that is the new heaven and new earth. Is this the story celebrated and sermonized in open and affirming churches? What about twenty years from now? And

---

[3] Gary Dorrien, *The Making of American Liberal Theology: Imagining Progressive Religion 1805–1900* (Louisville, KY: Westminster John Knox Press, 2001), xxiii.

what if we flesh out the story and include the hard bits about the exclusivity of Christ and the eternality of hell? What if part of the story is believing that every little jot and tittle in the Storybook is completely true? What if the story summons us to faith *and* repentance? What if the story centers on the cross, not supremely as an example of love, but as Love's objective accomplishment in the pouring out of divine wrath upon a sin-bearing substitute?

The support for homosexual behavior almost always goes hand in hand with the diluting of robust, 100-proof orthodoxy, either as the cause or the effect. The spirits which cause one to go wobbly on biblical sexuality are the same spirits which befog the head and the heart when it comes to the doctrine of creation, the historical accuracy of the Old Testament, the virgin birth, the miracles of Jesus, the resurrection, the second coming, the reality of hell, the plight of those who do not know Christ, the necessity of the new birth, the full inspiration and authority of the Bible, and the centrality of a bloody cross. Can someone deny that homosexual behavior is a sin and still believe every line in the Apostles' Creed or the Nicene Creed? Maybe . . . for a time . . . loosely. But as the cultural pressure gets harder and our handling of Scripture gets softer, will we still acknowledge, as the Athanasian Creed does, that "it is necessary for eternal salvation that one also believe in the incarnation of our Lord Jesus Christ," that "at his coming all people will arise bodily and give an accounting of their own deeds," that "those who have done good will enter eternal life, and those who have done evil will enter eternal fire," and that all this (including an orthodox understanding of the Trinity and the two natures of Christ) is "the catholic faith" and that "one cannot be saved without believing it firmly and faithfully"? What will it profit a man if he gains a round of societal applause but loses his soul?

We Have Seen His Glory

> And the Word became flesh and dwelt among us, and we have seen his glory, glory as of the only Son from the Father, full of grace and truth. (John 1:14)

Jesus was all grace and all truth, all the time. He welcomed sinners and tax collectors. He healed lepers and the lame. He had compassion on the crowds when they were hungry and far from home. He condemned self-righteous hypocrites. He prophesied judgment on Jerusalem for their unrepentant hearts. He talked about hell more than heaven. He obeyed the law and had mercy on lawbreakers. He gives everything to us and demands everything from us. He died for our sakes, and then told us we had to die for his.

We desperately need grace in our lives. We need to hear from Jesus, "Come to me, all you who are weary and heavy laden, and I will give you rest" (Matt. 11:28). We need to know that God doesn't expect us to clean up our act before we come to him. He implores us to come, now, today, just as we are—in brokenness, in pain, in humility, in repentance, and in faith. We need to hear that wayward children, who have squandered their inheritance and lived an immoral, rebellious life, can come home into the arms of their heavenly Father (Luke 15:20).

And we desperately need truth in our lives. We need to hear from Jesus, "The truth will set you free" (John 8:32). And we need to hear from Jesus what this saying really means: "Truly, truly, I say to you, everyone who practices sin is a slave to sin. . . . So if the Son sets you free, you will be free indeed" (John 8:34–36). We need someone as gracious as Jesus to tell us the truth: we are not OK. We need forgiveness. We need rescue. We need redemption.

We need truth. We need grace. We need Jesus.

Only Jesus can save a wretch like me. That's the storyline

of the Bible and the best news you'll ever hear. Jesus saves sinners—the cowardly and the cantankerous, the loveless and the lawless, the rude and the reckless, the adulterous and the idolatrous, the sexually proud and the sexually impure. Only in Jesus can we be given new birth. Only through Jesus can we be new creations. Only with Jesus can all things be made new. And only by listening to Jesus—and the book his Spirit inspired—will we come to realize that sometimes the new things are found only by sticking to the old paths (Jer. 6:16).

Appendix 1

What about Same-Sex Marriage?

By design, this book has been about the Bible. For the most part, I've stayed away from the legal, political, scientific, cultural, and educational controversies surrounding homosexuality. But in this appendix I want to briefly touch on the topic of same-sex marriage.

I debated whether to include this section. On the one hand, achieving some legal and political end is not the point of the book. My concern is with the church—what she believes, what she celebrates, and what she proclaims. And yet, I'm concerned that many younger Christians—ironically, often those most attuned to societal transformation and social justice—do not see the connection between a traditional view of marriage and human flourishing. Many Christians are keen to resurrect the old pro-choice mantra touted by some Catholic politicians: personally opposed, but publicly none of my business. I want Christians to see why this issue matters and why—if and when same-sex marriage becomes the law of the land—the integrity of the family will be weakened and the freedom of the church will be threatened.

I know this is an increasingly unpopular line of reasoning, even for those who are inclined to accept the Bible's teaching about marriage. Perhaps you agree with the exegetical conclusions reached in this book and believe that homosexual behavior is biblically unacceptable. And yet, you wonder what's wrong with supporting same-sex marriage as a legal and political right. After all, we don't have laws against gossip or adultery or the worship of false gods. Even if I don't agree with it, shouldn't those who identify as gay and lesbian still have the same freedom I have to get married?

That's a good question, but before we try to answer it, we need to be sure we are talking about the same thing. Let's think about what is *not* at stake in the debate over same-sex marriage.

- The state is *not* threatening to criminalize homosexual behavior. Since the Supreme Court struck down antisodomy laws in *Lawrence v. Texas* (2003), same-sex sexual behavior has been legal in all fifty states.
- The state is *not* going to prohibit those in homosexual relationships from committing themselves to each other in public ceremonies or religious celebrations.
- The state is *not* going to legislate whether two adults can live together, profess love for one another, or express their commitment in ways that are sexually intimate.

The issue is not about controlling "what people can do in their bedrooms" or "who they can love." The issue is about what sort of union the state will recognize as marriage. Any legal system which distinguishes marriage from other kinds of relationships and associations will inevitably exclude many kinds of unions in its definition. The state denies marriage licenses to sexual threesomes. It denies marriage licenses to eight-year-olds. There are an almost infinite number of friendship and kinship combinations which the state does *not* recognize as marriage. The state doesn't tell us who we can be friends with or who we can live with. You can have one friend or three friends or a hundred. You can live with your sister, your mother, your grandfather, your dog, or three buddies from work. But these relationships—no matter how special—have not been given the designation "marriage" by the church or by the state. The state's refusal to recognize these relationships as marital relationships does not keep us from pursuing them, enjoying them, or counting them as significant.

Marriage: What's the Big Deal?

In the traditional view, marriage is the union of a man and a woman. That's what marriage is, before the state confers any benefits on it. Marriage, in the traditional view, is a *prepolitical institution*. The state doesn't determine what defines marriage; it only recognizes marriage and privileges it in certain ways. It is a sad irony that those who support same-sex marriage on libertarian grounds are actually ceding to the state a vast amount of heretofore unknown power. No longer is marriage treated as a prepolitical entity which exists independent of the state. Now the state defines marriage and authorizes its existence. Does the state have the right, let alone the competency, to construct and define a society's most essential relationships?

We must consider why the state has bothered to recognize marriage in the first place. What's the big deal about marriage? Why not let people have whatever relationships they choose and call them whatever they want? Why go to the trouble of sanctioning a specific relationship and giving it a unique legal standing? The reason is that the state has an interest in promoting the familial arrangement whereby a mother and a father raise the children that came from their union. The state has been in the marriage business for the common good and for the well-being of the society it is supposed to protect. Kids do better with a mom and a dad.[1] Communities do better when husbands and wives stay together. Hundreds of studies confirm both of these statements (though we all can think of individual exceptions I'm sure).[2] Same-sex marriage assumes that marriage is redefinable and the moving parts replaceable.

By recognizing same-sex unions as marriage, just like the husband-wife relationship we've always called marriage, the state is engaging in (or at least codifying) a massive reengineering of our social life. It assumes the indistinguishability of gender in parenting, the relative unimportance of procreation in marriage, and the near infinite flexibility as to what sorts of structures and habits lead to human flourishing.[3]

But What about Equal Rights?

How can I say another human being doesn't have the same right I have to get married? That hardly seems fair. It's true: the right to marry is fundamental. But to equate the previous sentence with a right to *same-sex* marriage begs the question. It assumes that same-sex partnerships actually constitute a marriage. Having the right to marry is not the same as having a right to the state's validation that each and every sexual relationship is marriage. The

---

[1] See Katy Faust's striking article, "Dear Justice Kennedy: An Open Letter from the Child of a Loving Gay Parent," in which she maintains that she is "one of many children with gay parents who believe we should protect marriage" because "the government's interest in marriage is about the children that only male-female relationships can produce." *Public Discourse*, February 2, 2015, www.thepublicdiscourse.com/2015/02/14370.

[2] See Maggie Gallagher, "(How) Does Marriage Protect Child Well-Being?" in *The Meaning of Marriage: Family, State, Market, and Morals*, eds. Robert P. George and Jean Bethke Elshtain (Dallas: Spence, 2006), 198–200.

[3] For the best explanation of what marriage is, from the perspective of reason and natural law, see Patrick Lee and Robert P. George, *Conjugal Union: What Marriage Is and Why It Matters* (Cambridge: Cambridge University Press, 2014); Anthony Esolen, *Defending Marriage: Twelve Arguments for Sanity* (Charlotte, NC: Saint Benedict Press, 2014); Sherif Girgis, Ryan T. Anderson, and Robert P. George, *What Is Marriage? Man and Woman: A Defense* (New York: Encounter Books, 2012).

issue is not whether to expand the number of persons eligible to participate in marriage, but whether the state will publicly declare, privilege, and codify a different way of defining marriage altogether. Or to use a different example, the pacifist has a right to join the army, but he does not have the right to insist that the army create a nonviolent branch of the military for him to join.[4]

Redefining marriage to include same-sex partnerships publicly validates these relationships as bona fide marriage. That's why the state sanction is so critical to same-sex marriage proponents and so disconcerting to those with traditional views. The establishment of gay "marriage" enshrines in law a faulty view of marriage, one that says marriage is essentially a demonstration of commitment sexually expressed. In the traditional view, marriage was ordered to the well-being of the child, which is why the state had a vested interest in regulating and supporting it. Under the new morality, marriage is oriented to the emotional bond of the couple. The slogan may say "keep the government out of my bedroom," as if personal choice and privacy were the salient issues, but same-sex marriage advocates are not asking for something private. They want public recognition. I don't doubt that for most same-sex couples the longing for marriage is sincere, heartfelt, and without a desire to harm anyone else's marriage. And yet, same-sex unions cannot be accepted as marriage without devaluing all marriages, because the only way to embrace same-sex partnerships as marriage is by changing what marriage means altogether.

Enough Is Enough?

So why not call a truce on the culture war and let the world define marriage its way and the church define marriage its way?

---

[4] This analogy is taken from Voddie Baucham, "Gay Is Not the New Black," July 19, 2012, TGC, http://www.thegospelcoalition.org/article/gay-is-not-the-new-black.

You may think to yourself, maybe if Christians were more tolerant of other definitions of marriage, we wouldn't be in this mess. The problem is that the push for the acceptance of same-sex marriage has been predicated upon the supposed bigotry of those who hold a traditional view. The equal signs on cars and all over social media are making a *moral* argument: those who oppose same-sex marriage are unfair, uncivil, unsocial, undemocratic, un-American, and possibly even inhumane. If Christians lose the cultural debate on homosexuality, we will lose much more than we think. David S. Crawford is right:

> The tolerance that really is proffered is provisional and contingent, tailored to accommodate what is conceived as a significant but shrinking segment of society that holds a publically unacceptable private bigotry. Where over time it emerges that this bigotry has not in fact disappeared, more aggressive measures will be needed, which will include explicit legal and educational components, as well as simple ostracism.[5]

We must not be naive. The legitimization of same-sex marriage will mean the de-legitimization of those who dare to disagree. The sexual revolution has been no great respecter of civil and religious liberties. Sadly, we may discover that there is nothing quite so intolerant as tolerance.[6]

Does this mean the church should expect doom and gloom? That depends. For conservative Christians the ascendancy of same-sex marriage will likely mean marginalization, name-calling, or worse. But that's to be expected. Jesus promises us no better than he himself received (John 15:18–25). The church

---

[5] David S. Crawford, "Mechanism, Public Reason, and the Anthropology of Orientation: How the Debate over 'Gay Marriage' Has Been Shaped by Some Ubiquitous but Unexamined Assumptions," *Humanum* (Fall 2012): 8; available online at http://humanumreview.com//uploads/pdfs/CRAWFORD_SSU_main_17pp_(final).pdf.

[6] See D. A. Carson's excellent book, *The Intolerance of Tolerance* (Grand Rapids, MI: Eerdmans, 2012).

is sometimes the most vibrant, the most articulate, and the most holy when the world presses down on her the hardest.

But not always—sometimes when the world wants to press us into its mold, we jump right in and get comfy. I care about the decisions of the Supreme Court and the laws our politicians put in place. But what's much more important to me—because I believe it's more crucial to the spread of the gospel, the growth of the church, and the honor of Christ—is what happens in our local congregations, our mission agencies, our denominations, our parachurch organizations, and in our educational institutions. I fear that younger Christians may not have the stomach for disagreement or the critical mind for careful reasoning. Look past the talking points. Read up on the issues. Don't buy every slogan and don't own every insult. The challenge before the church is to convince ourselves as much as anyone that believing the Bible does not make us bigots, just as reflecting the times does not make us relevant.

Appendix 2

Same-Sex Attraction: Three Building Blocks

There is a growing discussion among those who agree that the Bible forbids homosexual practice about whether same-sex attraction itself is sinful. The issue requires careful thought, not least of all in defining our terms. What do we mean by words like *orientation*, *attraction*, and *desire*? What do others mean when they use these words? What does the Bible say, if anything, about what they should mean? While much of the underlying exegetical and theological work has a long history, the question itself is very new. It has come to special prominence as more and more Christians who experience same-sex attraction are, in a powerful picture of God's grace, choosing to live celibate lives rather than violate the clear teaching of Scripture.

More work needs to be done to help Christians think through the issue of same-sex attraction in a way that is biblically faithful, pastorally sensitive, and culturally conversant. I confess that I don't have all the answers, nor am I even sure of all the questions. But perhaps these building blocks—using the three categories I just mentioned—might help lay a good foundation for further reflection and application.

Block 1: Biblically Faithful

Whenever same-sex attraction manifests itself in "lustful intent," the desire is sinful, just as it would be for someone attracted to persons of the opposite sex (Matt. 5:28). That much is clear. But might there be some neutral ground of approval or approbation that falls short of sinful desire? I think so. A brother may be able to discern that his sister is beautiful, or a grown daughter may be able to recognize that her dad is handsome, without committing any of the wrong kind of *epithymia* (desire). In the same way, the person with same-sex attraction may be able to apprehend someone of the same sex as beautiful or handsome without moral culpability. But let's be careful: sinful desires aren't always as obvious as the articulated thought, "I wish I could have sex with this person." Sinful desires bubble up in long looks, second glances, entertainment choices, unhealthy emotional attachments, daydreams, and wandering eyes (Job 31:1). This goes for all of us, no matter our orientation.

As for the particularities of same-sex attraction, given the exegesis in this book we have to conclude that even unwanted homosexual desires are disordered (and if the desire is tantamount to "lustful intent," then sinful). That is, as one friend who experiences same-sex attraction put it, same-sex attraction—used here to mean more than men simply desiring the company of other men or women of women—did not exist before the fall, comes as a result of it, and will not exist when the fall has been finally overcome. Desires are deemed good or bad not just by their intensity or sense of proportion, but based on their object. For a man to desire to have sex with another man (or a woman with a woman) is not the way things are supposed to be.

Block 2: Pastorally Sensitive

But that's not all we must say. If we stop here, we will crush the spirits (or worse) of brothers and sisters who experience same-sex attraction through no conscious choice of their own. Every Christian wrestles with thoughts we can't quite understand and feelings we never wanted. This is not a homosexual problem; it's a human problem. I imagine a young man coming up to me as his pastor and saying, through tears, "I find myself attracted to men instead of women. I feel so dirty. I'm so ashamed. I feel bad, miserable, and mad at myself and like a failure before God every second of the day." In this situation I would eventually get to the call of Christian discipleship to live in purity of thought and deed, but that's not where I would start because this man already feels impure. I'd tell him that feeling this does not make him a failure, and that the desire to walk in holiness is evidence of the Spirit's work in his life. I'd tell him about the good news of the gospel. I'd tell him that I'm not the way I'm supposed to be either. I'd tell him that Jesus is a sympathetic high priest, that he intercedes for us, that he knows what it's like to be tempted and tried. I'd tell him that God gives us limps and thorns for our good and for his glory. I'd tell him that God can use our struggles to bless us and to bless others through us. If the person coming to me were a fifty-year-old planning to leave his wife and kids to run off with another man, my counsel might sound much different, but for the honest struggler we want to emphasize that disordered desires can arise in us unbidden and that finding yourself attracted to persons of the same sex does not destine you for a lifetime of guilt and self-loathing.

Block 3: Culturally Conversant

This is where the conversation gets even trickier because we aren't just dealing with what the Bible says or what we should say but what the wider world thinks we are saying with the words we say. Again, defining our terms is crucial, as is discerning how others are using the same terms. It's true (and a sometimes overlooked point) that terms like *orientation* and *gay* are used to signify much more than sexual activity or sexual desire. They may speak to a person's preference for same-sex friendship, or a person's place in much-needed community, or a person's delight in same-sex camaraderie and conversation. When people speak of "orientation" or "being gay," they may be speaking of much more than sex. But we must also bear in mind that the world probably doesn't hear *less* than sex when we use these terms. For this reason, I prefer to speak of "same-sex attraction" or Rosaria Butterfield's (not quite identical) phrase "unwanted homosexual desires." However we parse out these terms—and we cannot avoid parsing terms (new terms are probably needed too)—we must at least be clear about what we mean when we talk about matters so emotionally charged and verbally complex.

In the years ahead the church will be forced to think through these issues, think of them often and then act. The church will have a tremendous *opportunity* to be slow to speak and quick to listen, to keep our Bibles open and our hearts too, and to speak the truth in love and show truth and grace. Let's pray that we are up to the challenge and ready for the opportunity.

Appendix 3

The Church and Homosexuality: Ten Commitments

Of the many complexities involving the church and homosexuality, one of the most difficult is how the former should speak of the latter. Even for those Christians who agree that homosexual practice is contrary to the will of God, there is little agreement on *how* we ought to speak about it being contrary to the will of God. Much of this disagreement exists because we have many different constituencies in mind when we broach the subject. There are various groups that may be listening when we speak about homosexuality, and the group we think we are addressing usually dictates how we speak.

- If we are speaking to cultural elites who despise us and our beliefs, we want to be bold and courageous.
- If we are speaking to strugglers who fight against same-sex attraction, we want to be patient and sympathetic.

- If we are speaking to sufferers who have been mistreated by the church, we want to be winsome and humble.
- If we are speaking to shaky Christians who seem ready to compromise the faith for society's approval, we want to be persuasive and persistent.
- If we are speaking to those who are living as the Scriptures would not have them live, we want to be straightforward and earnest.
- If we are speaking to belligerent Christians who hate or fear persons who identify as gay or lesbian, we want to be clear and corrective.

So how ought we to speak about homosexuality? Should we be defiant and defensive or gentle and entreating? Yes and yes. It depends on who is listening. All six scenarios above are real and not uncommon. And while some Christians may be called to speak to one group in particular, we must keep in mind that in this technological day and age anyone from any group may be listening in. This means that we will often be misunderstood. It also means we should make some broad basic commitments to each other and to our friends and foes in speaking about homosexuality.

Here are ten commitments I hope Christians and churches will consider making in their heads and hearts, before God and before a watching world.

1. We will encourage our leaders to preach through the Bible verse by verse and chapter by chapter that they might teach the whole counsel of God (even the unpopular parts) and avoid riding hobby horses (even popular ones).
2. We will tell the truth about all sins, including homosexuality, but especially the sins most prevalent in our communities.

3. We will guard the truth of God's Word, protect God's people from error, and confront the world when it tries to press us into its mold.

4. We will call all people to faith in Christ as the only way to the Father and the only way to have eternal life.

5. We will speak to all people about the good news that Jesus died in our place and rose again so that we might be set free from the curse of the law, saved from the wrath of God, and welcomed into the holy city at the restoration of all things.

6. We will treat all Christians as new creations in Christ, reminding each other that our true identity is not based on sexuality or self-expression but on our union with Christ.

7. We will extend God's forgiveness to all those who come in brokenhearted repentance, everyone from homosexual sinners to heterosexual sinners, from the proud to the greedy, from the people pleaser to the self-righteous.

8. We will ask for forgiveness when we are rude or thoughtless or joke about those who experience same-sex attraction.

9. We will strive to be a community that welcomes all those who hate their sin and struggle against it, even when that struggle involves failures and setbacks.

10. We will seek to love all in our midst, regardless of their particular vices or virtues, by preaching the Bible, recognizing evidences of God's grace, pointing out behaviors that dishonor the Lord, taking church membership seriously, exercising church discipline, announcing the free offer of the gospel, striving for holiness together, practicing the "one anothers" of Christian discipleship, and exulting in Christ above all things.

Annotated Bibliography

If you want to keep exploring what the Bible says about homosexuality, you may want to check out some of the books on the list below. All of them approach the issue from the historic Christian position (or, in the case of some of the natural law books, reach conclusions consistent with the ones reached in this book). I've limited the list to recently published books, mainly those which have come out in the last two or three years. I do not pretend to provide an exhaustive list, but hopefully it is a representative list—the sort of bibliography that helps you know where to go for further study.

Biblical and Pastoral

INTRODUCTORY

Allberry, Sam. *Is God Anti-Gay? And Other Questions about Homosexuality, the Bible and Same-Sex Attraction.* Purcelville, VA: The Good Book Company, 2013. Short, personable, winsome. This is a book you can give to people on either side of this issue.

Barr, Adam T., and Ron Citlau. *Compassion without Compromise: How the Gospel Frees Us to Love Our Gay Friends without Losing the Truth.* Bloomington, MN: Bethany House, 2014. Good on application and how to think through real-life scenarios.

Hubbard, Peter. *Love into Light: The Gospel, the Homosexual, and the Church.* Greenville, SC: Ambassador International,

2013. Speaks to lonely strugglers and the Christians who need to learn to love them.

INTERMEDIATE

Burk, Denny. *What Is the Meaning of Sex?* Wheaton, IL: Crossway, 2013. Excellent overview of a big subject.

Thomas E. Schmidt. *Straight and Narrow: Compassion and Clarity in the Homosexuality Debate.* Downers Grove, IL: InterVarsity Press, 1995. A scholarly and accessible presentation of the most important material across several disciplines.

ADVANCED

Gagnon, Robert A. J. *The Bible and Homosexual Practice: Texts and Hermeneutics.* Nashville, TN: Abingdon Press, 2001. By all accounts, the most comprehensive and most detailed defense of the historic Christian position.

Apologetics and Natural Law

INTRODUCTORY

Heimbach, Daniel. *Why Not Same-Sex Marriage? A Manual for Defending Marriage against Radical Deconstruction.* Sisters, OR: Trusted Books, 2014. A big book, but in an easy-to-use format.

McDowell, Sean, and John Stonestreet. *Same-Sex Marriage: A Thoughtful Approach to God's Design for Marriage.* Grand Rapids, MI: Baker, 2014. A helpful manual, which includes a number of interviews with important church leaders and thinkers.

INTERMEDIATE

Esolen, Anthony. *Defending Marriage: Twelve Arguments for Sanity.* Charlotte, NC: Saint Benedict Press, 2014. Well written and provocative.

George, Robert P., and Jean Bethke Elshtain, eds. *The Meaning of Marriage: Family, State, Market, and Morals*. Dallas, TX: Spence, 2006. An impressive collection of essays on marriage and culture issues, including chapters on law, divorce, same-sex marriage, and the well-being of children.

ADVANCED

Girgis, Sherif, Ryan T. Anderson, and Robert P. George. *What Is Marriage? Man and Woman: A Defense*. New York: Encounter Books, 2012. Argues from natural law for the conjugal view of marriage.

Lee, Patrick, and Robert P. George. *Conjugal Union: What Marriage Is and Why It Matters*. New York: Cambridge University Press, 2014. Similar in content and conclusion to the volume by Girgis, Anderson, and George, but less attuned to contemporary media and a bit more philosophical in tone.

Acknowledgments

I'm grateful for the wonderful church family at University Reformed Church. Their prayers and support are invaluable. Thanks to the elders for their flexibility with my schedule, and special thanks to my pastoral colleagues, Ben Falconer and Jason Helopolous, for keeping the plates spinning while I hid out in my study.

My assistant, Jenny Olson, was a constant help, especially in putting my notes in order. Andrew Wolgemuth is a terrific agent and encourager. I don't know how any Crossway book gets written without Justin Taylor's remarkable assistance (maybe they don't!). Thanks for being a great editor and a better friend.

A number of very bright and very busy people took time to read my first draft: Sam Allberry, Matt Anderson, Ron Belgau, Denny Burk, Rosaria Butterfield, Kyle Keating, Andy Naselli, Andrew Wilson, Christopher Yuan, and one reviewer who preferred not to be named. I'm still to blame for the mistakes, of course, and I'm sure some of the reviewers still don't agree with everything I've written, but their comments improved the book significantly. I'm extremely grateful.

My kids—Ian, Jacob, Elsie, Paul, Mary, and Benjamin—lifted my spirits when the project dragged on. My wife Trisha is simply the best. All the time. I didn't deserve to hit the marital jackpot.

Scripture Index

Download a **FREE STUDY GUIDE** for

What Does the Bible Really Teach about Homosexuality?

at crossway.org/DeYoung2015

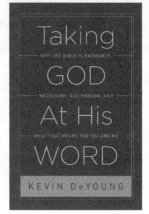